THE OBERON ANTHOLOGY OF CONTEMPORARY GREEK PLAYS

T0314873

THE OBERON ANTHOLOGY OF CONTEMPORARY GREEK PLAYS

L. Kitsòpoulou ◊ N. Rapi
Y. Mavritsakis ◊ A. Dimou
Ch. Giannou

OBERON BOOKS
LONDON

WWW.OBERONBOOKS.COM

This collection first published in 2017 by Oberon Books Ltd
521 Caledonian Road, London N7 9RH
Tel: +44 (0) 20 7607 3637 / Fax: +44 (0) 20 7607 3629
e-mail: info@oberonbooks.com
www.oberonbooks.com

First published in the Greek language by Sokolis Publications

M.A.I.R.O.U.L.A. [M.A.I.P.O.Y.Λ.A.] copyright © Lena Kitsopoulou, 2009*

This translation of *M.A.I.R.O.U.L.A. [M.A.I.P.O.Y.Λ.A.]* copyright ©
Aliki Chapple, 2012*

Angelstate [Angelstate] copyright © Nina Rapi, 2015*

This translation of *Angelstate [Angelstate]* copyright © Nina Rapi, 2017*

Wolfgang [Wolfgang] copyright © Yannis Mavritsakis, 2007*

This translation of *Wolfgang [Wolfgang]* copyright © Christina Polyhroniou, 2008*

Hungry [Πείνα] copyright © Charalampos Giannou, 2016*

This translation of *Hungry [Πείνα]* copyright © Charalampos Giannou, 2016*

... and Juliet [... και Ιουλιέτα] copyright Akis Dimou, 1995*

This translation of *... and Juliet [... και Ιουλιέτα]* copyright © Elizabeth Sakellaridou,
2017*

indicates year of first publication/performance

Lena Kitsopoulou, Nina Rapi, Yannis Mavritsakis, Akis Dimou and Charalampos
Giannou are hereby identified as authors of these plays in accordance with section
77 of the Copyright, Designs and Patents Act 1988. The authors have asserted
their moral rights.

Aliki Chapple, Nina Rapi, Christina Polyhroniou, Elizabeth Sakellaridou
and Charalampos Giannou are hereby identified as translators of these plays
in accordance with section 77 of the Copyright, Designs and Patents Act 1988.
The translators have asserted their moral rights.

A catalogue record for this book is available from the British Library.

PB ISBN: 9781783197675
E ISBN: 9781783197682

Designed by Konstantinos Vasdekis

eBook conversion by Lapiz Digital Services, India.

Visit www.oberonbooks.com to read more about all our books and to buy them.
You will also find features, author interviews and news of any author events,
and you can sign up for e-newsletters so that you're always first to hear about
our new releases.

Contents

Mapping Contemporary Greek Dramaturgy: 2000-2016
by George P. Pefanis

translated by Nina Rapi

Mapping and periodising dramaturgy are two challenging ventures, at times complementary but often contradictory. Their complementarity is apparent: local geographies are reflected in the histories of the people inhabiting them and mapping dramaturgy presupposes, somehow, an ordering of the mapped texts into a regime of historicity. Inaccuracies however may arise from this necessary process of connecting the present with the past, i.e. combining mapping with periodising. Theatre historians, therefore, should carefully consider these inaccuracies, something I shall endeavour to do here.

I believe that every return to the past is significant and imperative as it indicates a continuity, a connection with that to which I return. This is the meaning of 'historicity'. Naturally, the return assumes a starting point, a moment in the present and a social situation, from which I decide to return. To return where? Why should I return, for what purpose? How should I return, following which methodology, utilising what institutions, conceptualising on what ideological basis and making what aesthetic choices? The answers to these questions frame the decision of returning and determine the meaning of 'regime' in the regimes of historicity – created in the double movement of 'horizontal' and contemporary recording and evaluating of texts on the one hand, and their 'vertical', inter-temporal and inter-textual study and interpretation on the other: retrospection and presence in the here and now, returning to the past and bringing it alive in the present.

Consequently, the regime of historicity deduced before each combination of mapping and periodising proposes the formation of a tight sequence of temporal layers, during which the past is repossessed and reshaped continuously through the present, while the present obtains its distinctiveness through this very repossession and reshaping of the past.

In other words, the regime of historicity asserts the dynamic relationship between temporal/historical layers and their reproductions in the present,[1] involving a wider conception of time, an architecture of time.[2] Mapping and periodising theatre is therefore necessarily and closely connected to historical consciousness (awareness of history is probably the most significant revolution, according to Gadamer).[3]

Connecting the Past with the Present

Having presented these introductory thoughts, we may now attempt an overview of contemporary Greek dramaturgy. This naming which is both a temporal signifier and a summary categorization, inevitably discoursing with the past, offers us examples, motifs and principles for a deeper understanding of the contemporary, thus exploring the boundaries of both as fluid and permeable.

This can be seen in the context of research focused on the plays of a playwright whose writing activities extend from the past into the present, like Dimitris Dimitriadis for example. His first play *The Price of Rebellion in the Black Market* was written in 1966 and was directed by Patrice Chéreau in 1968 at Théâtre d'Aubervilliers, while his two most recent plays *Troy* and *Triplet and Blockage*, were both written in 2014 and directed in 2015, the first one by Savvas Stoubos at Attis Theatre and the second one by Yiannis Skourletis at Thission Theatre.[4] Where should Dimitriadis' work

---

[1] François Hartog, *Regimes of Historicity: Presentism and Experiences of Time*, Columbia University Press, New York 2015, p. x-xviii, 9, passim

[2] Antonis Liakos, *Revelation, Utopia and History: The Transformations of Historical Consciousness*, Polis, Athens 2011, pp. 17 passim

[3] Hans-Georg Gadamer, *The Matter of Historical Consciousness*, Indiktos, Athens 1998, p. 35

[4] Dimitris Tsatsoulis, *The Theatre of Deprivation and Catastrophe*, Afterword in *Dimitris Dimitriadis*, Indiktos, Athens 2007, pp. 103-124; Dimitra Kondylaki, *Dimitris Dimitriadis. Exploring the Possibility of the Unexpected*, Nefeli, Athens 2015; Kaliopi Exarhou, *Dimitris Dimitriadis: The Theatre of Humanism*, Sokolis, Athens 2016

be placed? In the excluded past or in contemporary theatre? (Given the fact that his plays were not produced for twenty-seven years). The answer is not easily definable. In most of his work one can detect the same game of metamorphosis, the same corrosive repetition of motifs, interchangeability of roles, polymorphous desire, as well as destruction as the almost necessary ritual for the possibility of self-knowledge and experiencing the unexpected, a ritual which often reaches the forbidden, the exaggerated,[5] the unacceptable, even the non-performable.

Marios Pontikas is another good example. From his early plays in the seventies (*The Spectators, Look at Them, A Panoramic View of a Nightshift*) through to his most recent one *Neighing*[6] his writing is characterised by a 'chain reaction of aggressive gazes' which break up the concept of selfhood, question the idea of identity, undermine the authority of naming and therefore of logos itself. This applies even for those of his texts which had hurriedly been categorised as belonging to a narrow-defined realistic dramaturgical circle of the post-junta period.

It would also be inaccurate to distinguish between the early plays and those of the later period, thematically at least. Then as now, Pontikas traces the ruins of reason and within that, of human relics; only now he does so by revisiting ancient Greek myths, as in his plays *Laius' Murderer and the Crow*[7] (and *Neighing*), where the ruins exist in the very foundation of logos while the end can be traced to a primal source of hope. In the

---

[5] Dimitris Dimitriadis, *Theatre as Exaggeration. A Debatable Approach with a Debatable Conclusion*, in his book *Perpetual Army. A Theatrical Myth*, Diapyron, Athens 2012, pp. 95-117

[6] See Kety Diamantakou-Agathou, *From The Depths of Myth to the End of Logos* in the publication *Marios Pontikas, Neighing*, Mauve Skiouros, Athens 2015, pp. 10-15

[7] Kyriaki Petrakou, *About Marios Pontikas and his Plays Laius' Murderer and the Crow* in her book *Shapes and Images. From Romanticism to Postmodernism. Sixteen Studies on Modern Greek Theatre*, Papazisis, Athens 2015, pp. 483-502

depths of the writer's thoughts and "underneath the words he writes, we can discover the operating rationale of a distorted offshoot of the once optimistic historicism and virile positivism, but also the intrusive discourse of the corrupt political and media demagogy and the fake neo-liberal 'humanism' which constructs a generalised and puritanical concept of human beings (see: Western human beings) in order to suppress peoples' mourning cries (the way the sound of the trombone once did in his self-named play)."[8]

Loula Anagnostaki is another writer connecting the past with the present. Her work spans from 1965, when her three seminal plays *Overnight Stop*, *The City*, and *The Parade*, were presented at Theatro Technis by the legendary Karolos Koun, up to the noughties when Lefteris Voyiatzis directed her play *To You, Who Are Listening to Me* at Theatro Kykladon. With themes of otherness and memory,[9] possible parallel worlds emerge in an ambiguous reality, often threatened by invisible forces invading the familiar spaces of the characters.[10] Anagnostaki's dramaturgy which employs elliptical writing, often introverted, sometimes enigmatic, and full of dream-like content and images from the subconscious, has influenced and continues to influence the Greek theatrical scene, unifying temporal layers whilst maintaining the background of personal adventure and collective history.

In this cycle we must also refer to Andreas Staikos, who from the beginning of his writing journey (*Daedalus*, 1971) up to the

---

[8] George P. Pefanis, *Theatre Devotees and Philosophers. Tracing a Philosophy of Theatre*, Papazisis, Athens 2016, p. 201

[9] George P. Pefanis, *The Greek Emigrant Experience between 1945 and 1980* in *The Plays of Petros Markaris and Loula Anagnostaki*, Journal of Modern Greek Studies vol. 25, no 2, 2007, pp. 213-224 and *From Theatre as Heterotopia to Memory Theatre. Elements for a Poetics of Memory in the Dramaturgy of Loula Anagnostaki*, in his book *Spectres of Theatre. Scenes of Theory III*, Papazisis, Athens 2013, p. 267-303

[10] Elizabeth Sakellaridou, *Levels of Victimisation in the Plays of Loula Anagnostaki*, Journal of Modern Greek Studies 14:1, 1996, pp. 103-122

present, doesn't hesitate to turn his back on the topical version of reality and turn his gaze instead to deeper layers of the real, where he can seek roles, rehearsals, theatrical structures and transformations. When he engages with history (*1843*, 1990; *The Apple of Milos*,1996; *Napoleontia*, 2007) he is not exploring the effect of events but their theatricality – using them as settings in order to reveal the fluidity of situations and the theatricality of human relations. His style is characterized by deliberate repetitiveness, theatrical gestures, refined language, games of transformation, the masking of behavior and the disguising of our actions. The most Pirandelloesque of the Greek writers, he explores the huge subject of identity by often juxtaposing his characters with their lesser reflections, lost in nebulous situations, ambiguous erotic confessions and ironic word play.[11]

To conclude this cycle, we must also mention the following playwrights: Kostas Mourselas, Giorgos Dialegmenos, and Giorgos Skourtis, who are still active today. We must also pay tribute to Iakovos Kambanellis, Dimitris Kehaidis, Pavlos Matesis, Vassilis Ziogas, and Margarita Liberaki, who have died recently but have contributed enormously to the shaping of contemporary Greek dramaturgy. Regardless of whether their plays are still often performed or not, they offer a representative picture of the possibilities, even the philosophical depth, that Greek drama has acquired or may acquire in the future.

These observations are significant in every study of contemporary Greek dramaturgy for two reasons. Firstly, as we have already mentioned, because each mapping presupposes a process of periodization and therefore rethinking the concept of time. Secondly, because of the real danger of the extremist historical and dramatic presentism, i.e. the tendency to see only conflicts and discontinuities and to ignore continuities, connections and durations, in temporal reality. Also because of an interesting contradiction identified in the efforts of those theatre scholars

---

[11] Hara Babanikola-Georgopoulou, *Rules and Exceptions. Essays on Modern Greek Theatre*, Ellinika Grammata, Athens 1999, pp. 154-155. See also: Aphrodite Sivetidou, *The Spectacle of Silence in Andreas Staikos' Theatre*, Ellinika Grammata, Athens 2000

who cite the 'postmodern condition', or the meta-dramatic development of theatre, so as to brand in the same ideological formation or the same "horizon of meanings"[12] tendencies such as the increasing autonomy of individual performance/theatre arts, the dominance of the director/auteur or the decline of the dramatic text. This ignores the fact that the time where directors ruled in the theatre, or indeed where presentism was most powerful, has been through modernism and its offshoot movements and not during postmodernism and its meta-dramatic idioms.

From Realism to Postmodernism and Beyond

At this point, playwrights who emerged in the last decade of the twentieth century and are still active today, should be introduced. Two important citations here are Akis Dimou and Elena Penga. Dimou has had a strong presence on the stages of Athens and Thessaloniki from 1995, with his play ... and Juliet (included in this anthology), to the present with his most recent play, All that my Heart Can Take in the Storm, performed by Bijoux de Kant at Theatro Technis in 2016, an adaptation of the novel First Love (1920) by Yiannis Kondylakis. Dimou often explores literature theatrically, approaching literary texts in diverse ways: from adaptations (Withering Stains of Blood, 2007; Mrs Koula, 2010; Zorba, 2011), to complex inter-textual layered plays (Andromache or a Woman's Landscape in the Middle of the Night, 1999; Marguerite Gautier is Travelling Tonight, 2005; You don't say – Oresteia, the Next Generation, 2011).[13] In any case, what he aims to do is to transcend the boundaries of literary genres, thus allowing himself to enter into a dialogue with literary texts and making them his own.

[12] I use the term here as meant by Andrew Bowie in: The Philosophy of Performance and the Performance of Philosophy, Performance Philosophy 1, 2015, p. 55 <http://www.performancephilosophy.org/journal>

[13] See Lina Rosi, Akis Dimou's Dramaturgy <http://www.greektheatre.gr/public/gr/greekplay/index/reviewview/27>

Dimou's dramatic landscapes always have a realistic base, a 'story' originating in contemporary social reality or at least a recognisable reality. The realistic element however is often made strange, through dreamlike images alluding to internal worlds. The monologue, one of the most popular forms in Greek dramaturgy in fact, often appears in his work, adopting the technique of the imagined listener (the way we encounter it in Ritsos' poetic monologues).

During the nineties Penga was considered the main representative of postmodern writing in Greek dramaturgy. What she seeks in many of her plays is the theatrical anatomy of a historical web, often focusing directly or indirectly on a distinguished historical figure (*Kate Kolwicz Presents a Brief History of Art*, 1995; *Nelly's Takes her Dog for a Walk*, 2003) or a historical situation (*When Go-Go Dancers Go Dancing*, 2002; *Who Are Our New Friends*, 2006).

Her plays, which she often directs herself, take their final shape during rehearsals. Even so, the final form always leaves a sense of the elliptical, the incomplete, the off-centre. This results from the dramaturgical techniques the writer uses in most of her plays (*Phaedra or Alcestis*, 2002; *Woman and Wolf*, 2014; *Fear*, 2016): hybrid forms, inter-textual layers, discontinuities and cuts, multiple meanings in dialogue, breaking up the continuous action into smaller drama units, thematic recycling, intense use of collage and new technologies – all of which give a fluid image of reality and a fragmented narrative structure.

Her writing is an associative process, breaking up fixities. Penga, even when her subject allows her to (*The Emperor's New Clothes*, 1999) does not condemn but uses instead parody and sarcasm to disguise her anguish for the uncharted present, the undefined spaces, lost people.

Multiple Identities: Actors Writing Plays

It is worth noting that a significant number of new writers are also actors (Eleni Rantou, Michalis Reppas, Thodoris Atheridis, Dimitra Papadopoulou, Alexandros Rigas, and Yiannis Kalovrianos) some of whom also direct. This fact is interesting not only because it is an old tradition in Western theatre, actors transferring their stage knowledge onto paper, but also because these writers establish themselves as the initial point at which the word is creatively connected with the body, the fiction of writing with the factum of the stage. This mutuality of texts and bodies, supported by the continuous process of developing a play during rehearsals, nullifies the argument that strictly separates dramaturgy from stage action. The text is actually being written on the stage for the stage.

Panagiotis Mentis is a writer-actor connecting the older and the younger generations.[14] From his first play (*Playmobil*, 1989) to his most recent ones, he cultivates a realistic dramatic language focused on social realities (*National Gallery*, 2000; *Dot.gr*, 2009), confinement in family situations (*Anna, I said*, 1994; *Foreigners*, 2001; *Hidden Wound*, 1995; *Reality and Show*, 1997), and female psychological portraits and dysfunctional relationships between the sexes (*Women at Sea, Off base*, 2004; *Towards Alexandroupolis*, 2006; *Red Women*, 2007).

Chryssa Spilioti is another playwright who is also an actress (and director). She established herself as a writer in 1997 with the hugely successful *Who Discovered America*. The play achieves an anatomy of female psychology, through a tight structure and witty dialogue. Spilioti's plays often explore the woman's position in interpersonal and social relationships (*Aga Sfi and Fi*, 2003; *Doors*, 2014) while also engaging in political situations, raising issues of cultural and racial conflicts (*Ice and Fire*, 2007; *The Tiger's Eye*, 2012) or the economic marginalisation and social degradation of outsiders (*Who is Sleeping Tonight?* 2012).

---

[14] George P. Pefanis, *Between the White Page and the Stage. The Presence of Panagiotis Mentis in the Modern Greek Theater* in his book *The Sand of the Text. Aesthetic and Dramaturgical Issues in Greek Theatre*, Papazisis, Athens 2008, pp. 375-396

Yannis Mavritsakis is another playwright who worked as an actor up to 2003. Since then he has dedicated himself to dramaturgy and is considered one of the most significant playwrights of the last few years. His plays have been translated into many languages and performed in many theatres in Europe and the States. Boldly, with an authentic writer's voice, excellent knowledge of on-stage-communication and the dramatic art, Mavritsakis is hard to classify. He seeks poetry and freedom in form and expression, approaches methodically life and death issues (*Blind Spot*, 2006; *Vitrioli*, 2010), and without hesitation explores sensitive areas of private consciousness and social life (*Wolfgang*, 2007, included in this volume). Mavritsakis also imagines in an eschatological way the explosion of the universe as the natural consequence of the revolutionary destruction of the present world (*Redshift*, 2012). His plays invite inspired directing but also philosophical explorations (*Fucking Job*, 2008), a deeply political play about normativity and the dysfunctions of contemporary, bulimic society.[15]

Unclassifiable must also be applied to the work of Vassilis Mavrogeorgiou, who is also an actor and director, and founder of Skrow Theater. His plays are usually the product of collaboration with other actors during rehearsals and it is often hard to distinguish the real from the imagined within them. From his first play, *The Cockroach* (2005), which was very successful as a dadaist musical, to his most recent work, where he creates surreal scenes, playful situations, fairytale worlds of legends, popular mythologies but also historical truth. Using monologic or duologic forms, his texts emanate the aliveness of a child's painting (*Only the Truth*, 2006), the spontaneity of an adolescent (*A Huge Blast*, 2011) but also the melancholy of adult life (*Lions*, 2010 with K.Gaki). His play *The History of Self-sacrifice* (2014) contains all of these three elements and, although it is written with humour, it is a very serious examination of memory, as it gives moral authority to victims of society and to those 'heroes' that don't let death wait. The same applies to his most recent play *Damage: Things I Left Behind* (2016).

---

[15] George P. Pefanis, *Theatre Devotees and Philosophers*, ibid, pp. 121-164 & 263-272

The actress, director and short-story writer Lena Kitsopoulou, a rebellious, sarcastic, often aggressive voice, emerged as a dramatist in 2009 with *M.A.I.R.O.U.L.A.* (included in this volume), a sharp and self-deprecating monologue set against mundane daily life and contrasted with ideologies of a healthy relationship, a 'normal' way of living, a happy life. This play sets the tone for her next plays, through to her most recent one with the characteristic title: *One Day, Just Like Any Other Day...or The Vapidity of Being* (2015). Kitsopoulou targets violence in any form: from the debasement of language and national hysteria (*Aoustras or Couch Grass*, 2011), to the paranoia of family ties (*Neurosis*, 2012) and the terror of consumerism (*The Price*, 2012), to asserting that violence is actually within us (*Red Riding Hood – The First Blood*, 2014). Debunking myths, rejecting oppressive rules and doctrines, and exposing power in personal and collective life, her work has a strong political and critical core, presented through satire and parody.

Giorgos Iliopoulos also has multiple identities: he is an actor, a drama teacher, a writer and a director for the stage and screen. His first play *Desperados* was staged in 1998 and he has since maintained a steady presence on the Greek stage, as well as abroad. In his black comedies, his situation comedies (*The Catch*, 2009), but also in his more dramatic plays (*The Black Box*, 2006), his writing is comic but also melancholic, his language full of slang and idioms. His thematic concerns vary from the adventures and difficulties of sexual love (*4ever*, 1999; *Trolling*, 2014; *Speed Date*, 2016) to youth troubles (*The End of Summer*, 2000; *For Ever Starts Today*; 2009) to family dysfunctions (*Family Ties*, 2004).

Following the dramaturgy of actors, it is worth mentioning at least three examples of director-writers. First of all, *The National Hymn* (2001) by Mikhail Marmarinos, a work of great consequence both in postmodern Greek dramaturgy as well as in staging practice: "Through free associations, it transforms a static local symbol into a tool of theatre research, within and outside national boundaries."[16] Next, *Medusa* (2011) by Thomas Moschopoulos, one of the most important performances of the Athens and Epidaurus Festival, undertakes a deep rupture with the meaning of the past, lived experience and memory and unveils the anonymous, unjustly dead citizens, the 'wreckages' of human history, as described in *Theses on the Philosophy of History* by Walter Benjamin.[17] Finally, *fuck you euro, on your knees drachma, sing us a song too* (2015) by Vassilis Papavassiliou presents a deeply relevant, political, hilarious monologue, acted superbly by its writer/director.

Monologues: Internalising the Absence of the Other

The choice of monologue as a form, popular in Greece of late, may be argued to reflect the intense need for a more immediate address. Still, it is a complex phenomenon which cannot be fully analysed here. It is connected however with the search for dramatic texts which minimise the distances, encourage the development of new ways of narration, require the minimum possible production costs with the actor at its centre, and which explores the desire to internalise the absence of the Other (Vassilis Katsikonouris: *Harley's Jacket or It Could be Worse*, 2004; Dimitris Finitsis: *Silenced Mouth*, 2007). "The self-containment of the monologue play on stage reflects the loneliness of subjectivity in modern life. On the other hand it also offers a refuge for individual consciousness to live and express the desire for the absent listener."[18] Whether the monologue is by one character (*Almost Won* by Chryssa Spilioti,

---

[16] Kyriaki Frantzi, *Mikhail Marmarinos and the Cross-Cultural Dimension of the National Hymn*, M. Rossetto, M. Tsianikas, G. Couvalis & M. Palaktsoglou (eds.), *Greek Research in Australia: Proceedings of the Eighth Biennial International Conference of Greek Studies*, Flinders University, Department of Languages-Modern Greek, Adelaide 2009, (pp. 633-645), p. 634

[17] Walter Benjamin, *Sur le concept d'histoire*, *Œuvres III*, Gallimard, Paris 2000, pp. 427-443

[18] George P. Pefanis, *The Sand of the Text*, ibid, p. 421

2004; *M.A.I.R.O.U.L.A.* by Lena Kitsopoulou, 2009; *Medea's Burka* by Andreas Flourakis, 2010)[19] or for many characters (*Seven Logical Answers* by Leonidas Prousalidis, 2004; *The Gate Crashers* by Maria Evstathiadi, 2010; *Wild Beats* by Nina Rapi, 2014) the presence of the absent Other is a core dramaturgical tool which further allows autobiographical layers (*Dark Evenings* by Andreas Staikos, 2003; *La Poupee* by Vagelis Hatziyiannidis, 2008; *Fucking Job* by Yannis Mavritsakis, 2008) or philosophical and historical observations (*Disguise* by V. Hatziyiannidis, 2003; *A Seminar on Stupidity* by Sakis Serefas, 2008; *The Sixth Caryatid* by Antonis and Konstantinos Koufalis, 2010).

Family: The Difficulty of Living with the Other

The family, couples and sexual relationships continue to occupy thematically a significant part of contemporary Greek theatre, often with sharp and political undertones. If in the monologic form the Other is always present, in these plays what is emphasised is the difficulty of living with the Other. The Other is either departing (*There is no Home* by Antonis Nikolis, 2002; *Disobedience* by Maria Efstathiadi, 2003), goes to prison (*The Vest* by Vassilis Katsikonouris, 2004) or dies (*In One Hour* by Andreas Flourakis, 2001; *Melted Butter* by Sakis Serefas, 2007). Family ties, which have always been one of the strongest forces in Greek culture, seem to undergo a powerful crisis, equivalent to that of society in general at the beginning of the 21st century. Family is destroying her children (*The Mist* by Antonis and Konstantinos Koufalis, 2009; *Edgewise* by Nina Rapi, 2010) and is itself destroyed (*Hunger* by Charalampos Giannou, 2012, included in this volume).

Political Thoughts and Dystopias: at the Centre of Greek Dramaturgy

The modern capitalist world, with its inevitable inequalities and injustices, its accumulated wealth and marginalisation of people of low or no income, as well as the overall decrease of living standards, was and remains at the centre of Greek dramaturgy.

[19] Barbara Daliani, *Theatre Material. A Study on Andreas Flourakis' Dramaturgy*, Aparsis, Athens 2014

Maria Efstathiadi in her play *Privatopia* (2013) presents with spine-tingling accuracy the modern face of capitalism: on the one hand we see the private utopia of the rich, living within guarded walls, and on the other we witness the poor, the homeless and the immigrants. In between lies the media world and virtual reality.

Nina Rapi, an exciting new presence with sharp insights and an idiosyncratic aesthetic, in her play *Wild Beats* (2014) portrays the disciplining of art and the repression of its transgressive energy by invisible authorities, located in an unusual research centre. It is in fact a labyrinthine prison with corridors always leading back to the cell that the characters are trying to escape from. This centre, complex roles and dark memories from the dictatorship delineate the play's panopticon of contemporary power. The character resisting power here is a cult singer with a strong following while in *Kiss the Shadow* (2010) she is a radical composer disappearing in a border town in central Europe. The latter soon becomes a symbol of resistance and the investigation taking place to locate her cannot separate myth from reality. In *Reasons to Hide* (2009) the writer constructs a play with a strong political position against discipline and control "directing her fervour against targets which are not being named but are indeed identifiable".[20] For a politically aware writer, formed as a playwright in the oppositional circles of contemporary English dramaturgy, her targets are none other than violently imposed submission to political and sexual normativity.[21]

---

[20] Menelaos Karatzas, *Nina Rapi's Dramaturgy* <http://www.greek-theatre.gr/public/gr/greekplay/index/reviewview/16>

[21] On Nina Rapi see also: Margaret Rose, *Monologue Plays for Female Voices*, Tirrenia Stampatori, Italy, 1995, pp. 103-108; E. Goodman, *Modern Drama*, Volume XXXIX, Number 1, Spring 1996, pp. 193-196; Sandra Freeman, *Putting your Daughters on the Stage*, Cassell 1997, pp. 136-142; Dimple Godiwala-McGowan, *Alternatives Within the Mainstream II: Queer Theatre in Postwar Britain*, Cambridge Scholars Press, 2006, pp. 3-4; Samuelle Grassi, *Looking Through Gender: Post-1980 British and Irish Drama*, Cambridge Scholars Publishing, Cambridge 2011, pp. 87-93 & by the same author: in Silvia Antosa (ed.), *Queer Crossings. Theories, Bodies, Texts*, Mimesis, Milano 2012, pp. 179-192

Political dystopia has many faces in Greek dramaturgy. Vassilis Katsikonouris has depicted many of those. His realistic gaze confronts critically social situations without missing out the psychological aspects and specific personal conditions. His best known and most successful play *The Milk* (2003) takes place in a half-basement flat, lived in by immigrants from Tyflida, Georgia, where mental illness, obsessive memories, and addiction to childhood states of being become the mirror of social pathologies. Obsessive memories with their moral consequences also appear in *The Missing Ones: An Interesting Life* (2005), but with clear political references to the missing persons from the Turkish invasion of Cyprus.

Political thought, both dramaturgically and directorialy in the last few years, has often been expressed through the immigrant and the foreigner (*Unshaved Chins* and *Invisible Olga* by Yiannis Tsiros, 1996 and 2009 respectively; *Athens-Moscow* by Evdokimos Tsolakidis, 2002; *Who Are Our New Friends*, 2006 by Elena Penga; *Hair in My Soup* by Dimitris Generalis, 2008; *The Threat* by Artemis Moustaklidou, 2009; *The Yellow Dog* by Michel Fais, 2009 – based on the racist attack on Konstantina Kouneva, a Bulgarian activist, now a Greek M.P.; *Aoustras or Couch Grass* by Lena Kitsopoulou, 2011; *The Whole Town is Talking about It* by Antonis and Konstantinos Koufalis, 2013; *A Night at the Highway* by Lia Vitali, 2014; *Kangaroo* by Vassilis Katsikonouris, 2014).

Other focuses typically attributed to plays which are concerned with political thought include: the indifferent and apathetic citizen (*Belle Epoch* by Andreas Flourakis, 2012), a cannibalistic society (*The Big Game* by Lia Vitali, 2000; *Still Life. For the Glory of the City* by Manolis Tsipos, 2013[22]), the everyday exploitation of your fellow human being (*She Took Life Into Her Own Hands* by Vassilis Katsikonouris, 2007), the undermining of traditional national and moral values (*Wild Seed* by Yiannis Tsiros, 2013; *I Want a Country* by Andreas Flourakis, 2013), or

---

[22] Giorgos Sabatakakis, Afterword in: *Manolis Tsipos: Still Life: For the Glory of the City*, Gavriilidis, Athens 2015, pp. 59-64

finally the incapability or even unwillingness of the authorities to prevent injustice and political corruption (*Keep Your Eyes Open* and *Lectures on Degradation* by Yiannis Tsiros, 2007 and 2014 respectively).[23]

An Emerging Dramaturgy of Memory

It's not only that theatre is a memory machine,[24] but very often memory creates a dramatic structure. On the one hand there is *theatre memory,* seeking to temporarily halt the passing of time, to materialise the immaterial, to make present the 'no longer present'. On the other hand, there is *memory theatre* bringing alive the past through roles, the reproduction of concrete situations or recalling scenes from the past through corresponding present ones.[25] Greek dramaturgy develops increasingly and powerfully into a dramaturgy of memory.

In *Memories From The Sand* (2001) by Dimitris Kordatos, the father is a 'moving memorabilia' and the whole play consists of layers of memories, some of which are being recalled in order to prevent others from emerging. In *Addio del Passato* (2005) by Lia Vitali, the daughter is talking to her dead mother and in *Lisbon* (2005) by Antonis Nikolis, it is no longer certain whether we are witnessing the process of mourning, through reminiscing the dead, or a projection of the present on to the possible death of the living characters.

[23] Savvas Patsalidis and Anna Stavrakopoulou, *From the Years of Utopia to the Years of Dystopia*, Introduction to the Tribute: *The Geographies of Contemporary Greek Theatre. About Utopias, Dystopias and Heterotopias*, Gramma/Γράμμα journal vol. 22 (2), 2014, (pp. 7-16), pp. 11-16

[24] Marvin Carlson, *The Haunted Stage. The Theatre as Memory Machine*, The University of Michigan Press, Ann Arbor 2001

[25] George P. Pefanis, *Theatre Memory. Memory Locations in Modern Greek Dramaturgy,* in his book *Theatre Phantoms. Scenes of Theory III*, Papazisis, Athens 2013, pp. 210-266

In *The City On Her Knees* (2006) by Michel Fais, the past of a whole city is concentrated into a series of photos, where the homeless, the immigrants and the mentally ill are first displayed as images and then begin to come alive. It is often that photographs become the vehicle of memory like the digital optical spheres in *Midnight in a Perfect World* (2013) by Alexis Stamatis, where memory, the man's voice in the cassette tape, becomes the key to inspiration but also to personal pain, as it evokes guilt and activates trauma at a critical, existential time.

In *The Carriage in the Water* (2010) by Leonidas Prousalidis, the images created on stage are nothing but recollections coming alive as the heroine's dreams; and in his play *Air* (2011), Vagelis Hatziyiannidis traces the biography of a family through the memories of two sisters.

Taste, like the senses of vision and hearing, plays an active part in the drama of memory. In the awarded *Mam* (2006) by Sakis Serefas, food is the main source of memory recollection. The act of tasting something unlocks a memory associatively, thus proving to be a real life-school. When one eats they become one with what is on the table, even if it is served in modest tupperware by a school bus driver.

Often, the content of a private memory encounters an event from modern history. The monologue *Danube Trout* (2010) by Michel Fais explores the resurfacing of Jewish memories which causes a confession, mourning, and the realisation of the weight of time. Thanasis Triaridis' plays *Mengele* (2012), *Lebensraum* (2014), and *Zyklon or Fate* (2015) all engage with the horror of the holocaust as their historical backgrounds. Memory takes the form of role play but proves to be the determining factor for identifying the self (or an uncharted part of the self), and at the same time it becomes a nightmarish adventure, where the self is in danger of losing itself within the images generated by memory.

In *Angelstate* (2015) by Nina Rapi (included in this volume) six characters, each of whom is a strange mixture of the angelic and the demonic, live on the social margins and in an existential limbo, confined to 'a research centre/prison alluding to a mind-scape or the reverse'. The 'reverse' here could be perceived to be the context of a psychic panopticon or a political heterotopia where a faceless kind of authority enforces private confessions and extracts memories. The inflicted memories expose forgotten traumas in a dystopic setting of compulsory expiation, where old traumas define the present.

In the sense that the layering of memory presents the depth and intensity of Greek dramaturgy, the identification of inter-textual fields reveals the breadth, flexibility and open orientation towards theatre, literature, philosophy, theory and other art forms, both old and new. The inter-textuality of the plays, and the memory of the texts and their internal communication, goes beyond the hierarchical idea of influences; these are instead aspects of a dynamic relationship between reader and spectator, the text and the performance and assume an active participation in the meaning-creating process but also with the desire to open up to multi-faceted, polyphonic, elliptical and incomplete readings of the plays.[26] If dramatic texts can communicate with each other, if there is a secret memory in the plays which allow the reader/spectator to travel from play to play and performance to performance, then mapping and periodising lose their strict boundaries and open up to more dynamic intertextual fields.

Myths: Eternal Source of Inspiration

One of the strongest fields in Greek dramaturgy is that of plays exploring myths originating in ancient Greek drama. Beyond the key contributions to the genre by older writers (e.g. Ziogas, Matesis, Kabanellis, Dimitriadis,[27] Pontikas) we can selectively

---

[26] Dimitris Tsatsoulis, *Signs of Writing/Codes of Staging in Contemporary Greek Theatre*, Nefeli, Athens 2007, p. 53

[27] See Kety Diamantakou-Agathou, *From Théâtre de la Commune in 1968 to Théâtre Odéon in 2010: The Journey of Ancient Myth in the Theatre Work by Dimitris Dimitriadis* in the volume: *Scenic Action in Postwar Theatre: Continuities + Ruptures,* Archives from the International Scientific Conference, dedicated to Nikiforos Papandreou, Dept. of Theatre Studies, Aristotelio University of Thessaloniki, published by the University's Press, 2014, pp. 473-484

refer to the following newer plays: *Scottish Shower* (2000) by Chryssa Spilioti; *Babushka* (2002) by Vassilis Katsikonouris; *Cassie* (2003) and *Atreides, End* (2005) by Andreas Flourakis; *Oedipus, Anti-Oedipus* (2004) by Giorgos Veltsos, a metadramatic exploration of the philosophical approaches to the Oedipus myth; *The Frozen Garden* (2007) by Maria Efstathiadi, a modern synthesis of elements from Sophocles' and Pasolini's works; and *Helen's (eternal) Tragedy* (2014) by Dimitris Finitsis. These plays enrich an already huge post-mythic hypertext, which is of course still in development.

Additional Thematic Cycles

Although the inter-textual relationships in Greek plays cannot be easily categorised, we can identify four more thematic cycles. Firstly, plays that refer to other plays and writers e.g. *The Announcement. A Tribute to Strindberg* (2001) by Giorgos Veltsos and *Storm, Sabine X* (2007) by Manolis Tsipos, signaling amongst other texts *The Investigation* by Peter Weiss; *The Ninth Wedding* by Lia Vitali, which directly references Dürrenmatt's *The Visit*; *Hunger or Home* (2014) by Charalampos Giannou, with echoes from early Ziogas; *I, Gogo* (2013) by Eleni Gasouka, pointing to *Happy Days* by Beckett.

Secondly, plays drawing inspiration from literary figures, such as: *When Papadiamantis met Vizeynos* (2006) by Yiannis Soldatos; *Mud* (2008) by Vagelis Hatziyiannidis; *Poe* (2009) by Yiannis Soldatos; and *Demon, Sostenuto Assai Cantabile* (2010) by Maria Efstathiadi, based on *Demons* by Dostoyevsky.

Further, plays exploring philosophy: *Habemus Papam, Walter* (2008) by Manolis Tsipos for example, visualising the thought of Walter Benjamin; and the plays by philosophy professor Theodosis Pelegrinis who has written about a number of philosophers e.g. Heraclitus, Socrates, Descartes, Nietzsche, and Wittgenstein, over a number of years.[28]

---

[28] See Kyriaki Petrakou, *Philosophy on Stage and Stages in Philosophy: Theodosis Pelegrinis' Theatre* in her book *Shapes and Images: From Romanticism to Postmodernism*, Papazisis, Athens 2015, pp. 385-403

Finally, we can identify one more thematic unit which includes distinct references to music, films and the visual arts, such as: *Zebekiko* (2012) by Lia Vitali and *Rosa* (2012) by Panagiotis Mentis, both inspired by the lives of rebetika singers; *The Last Martha* by Alexis Stamatis, which focuses on a painting; and *Never Together* (2009) by Tzimaras Tsanatos based on the film *Gegen die Wand/Head On* by Fatih Akin.

Conclusion

This inclusive mapping focuses by necessity on certain aspects of contemporary Greek dramaturgy, presenting a wide sample of plays produced or published in Greece and abroad, mainly during the period 2000-2016, in an effort to introduce as many writers, plays and trends as possible. This essay cannot and does not claim to be *the* complete study of contemporary Greek dramaturgy but it is, hopefully, a good starting point for new researchers, together with other studies in the international bibliography.[29]

[29] I shall here only refer to recent tributes to contemporary Greek theatre by four prestigious scientific journals: Stratos E. Constantinidis and Walter Puchner (eds.), *Modern Greek Theater, Journal of Modern Greek Studies*, vol. 25, no 2, 2007; Georges P. Pefanis (ed.), *Perspectives du théâtre grec contemporain*, Annuaire Théâtral 48, 2010; Thèodoros Grammatàs and Gilda Tentorio (eds.) *Sguardi sul teatro greco contemporaneo*, Culture Teatrali 23, 2014; and Savvas Patsalidis, Anna Stavrakopoulou (eds.), *The Geographies of Contemporary Greek Theatre: About Utopias, Dystopias and Heterotopias*, Gramma/Γράμμα journal, vol. 22 (2), 2014

Also useful is the book by Kyriaki Petrakou: *The Impact of Modern Greek Theatre Abroad. Translations, Performances*, Ergo, Athens 2005. From the recent anthologies of modern Greek plays see: Theatre Lab (ed.), *Contemporary Greek Theatre*, vol. I, II, Arcadia, London 1999, 2002 and Myrto Gondicas (dir.), *Auteurs dramatiques grecs d'aujourd'hui. Miroirs tragiques, fables modernes*, (anthology), Les cahiers de la Maison Antoine Vitez, no 11, Éditions Théâtrales, Montreuil 2014. Finally a bibliography on Greek dramaturgy up to 2004 can be found in: George P. Pefanis, *Bibliographical Sources of Greek, Postwar Dramaturgy (1950-2004), The First Archive*, in his book *Texts and Meanings. Essays and Articles on Theatre*, Sokolis, Athens, 2005, pp. 153-212

We have of course seen from the beginning that the chronological developments cannot be ordered conceptually, neither can they offer substantive support to the meaning of *contemporary*, as the new/old are not necessarily historical entities but names given to a certain theoretical choice, if not an ideological prejudice. In my view, the meaning of the phrase 'contemporary Greek dramaturgy' does not refer to a relationship between mutually exclusive characteristics (contemporary versus old and irrelevant, active versus inactive), neither to a position of ordering a chronological (and therefore causal) sequence but to a dialectical interaction between that which has already taken place and that which is taking place now, a relationship which exposes the fluid character of temporal boundaries and definitions, reveals the inter-textual undercurrents of the plays and unveils the dynamics of the regimes of historicity.

Still, I believe that this particular period of our focus, beyond the fact that it coincides with what is commonly perceived as 'contemporary', can be examined independently in the sense that a) it includes the active participation of those writers who emerged in the Greek theatrical scene much earlier, b) the plays being written now present a number of formal and thematic influences from writers who are no longer alive, c) the writers who appear for the first time now are striving to develop their own voice and create their own theatrical space, and d) the financial crisis which started in 2009 and unfortunately still continues (2016) has deeply affected dramaturgical production. State funding of the theatre became problematic initially by being late on payments, later by reducing available funds and finally by abolishing them altogether.[30] Many theatres were forced, as a result, to limit or interrupt their activities and postpone or even cancel programmed productions of plays. The financial resources became hard to find and the available stages

---

[30] Regarding state funding of the theatre see Giorgos Sabatakakis, *Money and Theatre. State Funding in the 21st Century,* in the book by George P. Pefanis (ed.) *The Glamour of Money in Modern Greek Literature. From the Cretan Renaissance to the Beginning of the 21st Century,* Kostas and Eleni Ourani Foundation, Athens 2014, pp. 140-155

for new plays to be performed were drastically limited. Still, these difficulties have not prevented immense dramaturgical creativity, as shown here.

The fact that writers do not allow these financial difficulties to stop them from producing work and instead strive to create and adapt to these new conditions is a good indication that the dramaturgy of the previous decades has already created a 'tradition' which the younger ones somehow embrace and continue with a renewed energy, developing further the art of dramaturgy both thematically and formally.

George Pefanis is Associate Professor in Philosophy and Theory of Theatre and Drama at the Department of Theatre Studies, the National & Kapodistrian University of Athens, as well as a theatre critic.

M.A.I.R.O.U.L.A.
by Lena Kitsopoulou

Translated by Aliki Chapple

M.A.I.R.O.U.L.A.

The introductory stage direction in Lena Kitsopoulou's play sets a very specific context: a woman, a person of indefinable identity (except gender and age), in a flat, in a bourgeois setting; more specifically, in the kitchen, a room that is not in the least randomly chosen. The kitchen encompasses almost everything: it is the heart of the house, a point of reference for the family, an outdated symbol of women's position in society, a symbol of folk tradition. The kitchen carries a part of the Greek national identity and is at the same time a symbol of modern-life, material affluence.

When doing research for kitchen renovation, one usually comes across something like the following advertisement text: *The kitchen is that particular space in a house which most must satisfy our needs and meet our expectations. We know it must be pretty, functional, practical, effective and resistant. It must inspire us to be generous and caring, to have fun and feel relaxed. It has to inspire us to offer love.* What if we replaced the word kitchen in this ad with the word woman? How far is the picture described here from the various roles that women are expected to play in today's society? This is a rather disturbing coincidence – and quite deliberate, in my opinion.

Inside this closed room, the woman's monologue sweeps everything away from its path. It is as if her thoughts pour out fiercely through a window she has chosen to open with harsh candour, articulating all the things that cross our minds but we never dare to share. Her discourse is plain, unforced; her speech is breathless, with barely any full stops; it is caustic, sarcastic, sometimes even angry, but always poetic in essence. As her thoughts race through her mind, she moves from one subject to another at vertiginous speed and illuminates, with economy but also insight, a number of issues over which much ink has been spilt: modern-life depression, loneliness, problematic relationships, the pointlessness of existence, the stripping of folk wisdom, the demystification of love, all everyday minor compromises that lead us, with mathematical precision, to realizing the meaninglessness of life. Above all, she focuses on the human individual, who has convinced her-/himself that s/he can control everything s/he has set her/his mind on; the person who thinks that s/he is the centre of the universe; who wants to exorcise pain, sorrow, all intense emotions; who has discovered a clue to everything – to good health, longevity... even to happiness itself. She picks on the human individual, who is ultimately incapable of comprehending the meaning and purpose of life. But in the end, everything looks futile. Death is always there, lurking behind, reminding her/him that s/he is not invincible.

The heroine in Lena Kitsopoulou's monologue is walking towards the inevitable end of her life, while seeking ways of understanding who she is and how she can sustain her existence. Being the child of a society of superficial prosperity but rotten roots (let's not forget that the text was written right before the beginning of the economic crisis in Greece), the central character becomes the symbol of a generation that was born into and raised with ideas, attitudes and mentalities that do not match her desires in the least. She has been asked to believe in and function according to a philosophy of life that has nothing to do with her true needs. When all ideas and expectations prove false, how can life, possibly, have any meaning at all?

Kitsopoulou's heroine refuses to sit down and wait for the pointlessness of existence to be confirmed. She chooses to exorcise her biggest fear, death, by swallowing a tiny miracle pill called M.A.I.R.O.U.L.A. – an acronym that in Greek stands for: *Do Not Resist, Fall Flat, Go To Eternal Sleep, Redeem Yourself, Commit Suicide.* But ultimately, does this encounter with death bring any change at all? Or are we to conclude that all there is to live is right here?

Maria Karananou
Dramaturg and Head of Publications
for the National Theatre of Greece

M.A.I.R.O.U.L.A.: Notes on the translation

Mairoula (pronounced Meroula) is a name, an affectionate diminutive for Mairy (Mery) or Maria. It is presumably the character's name, though she never claims it. Mairi Protoppapa originated the role in Athens.

The original text of M.A.I.R.O.U.L.A. in Greek has very few stage directions, only a handful of full stops and barely so much as a paragraph break, being punctuated almost entirely with commas. For the reader's convenience, I have added paragraph breaks and some further punctuation, while retaining most of the original commas to convey the breakneck torrent of the monologue. The stage directions have simply been translated as they stand.

Translation is always interpretation, but with this text – ornamented, colourfully idiomatic, and sprinkled with literary references – it is particularly so. I have erred on the side of keeping it natural-sounding; this is a text for performance, and it needs to be utterable. Some jokes have been re-written to work in English, and some synonyms have been used where the original repeats a word, as Greek has a higher tolerance for repetition. I have also added a few glancing literary references, so that in English, as in Greek, the occasional familiar phrase peeks out.

Though the spelling is British, I have used mostly U.S idiom in this translation; "ass" instead of "arse", "couch" instead of "sofa", "discount store" and so forth. This is primarily because I am more familiar with such earthy language in U.S English and felt I could better convey the Greek in this way, and secondarily because I translated it in order to perform it myself in my own mid-Atlantic accent.

In a few places in the text I have interpolated, mostly a phrase explaining a Greek expression. These are marked by brackets. It is a translation decision made for the ease of readers unfamiliar with Greek culture, and I stand by it, as I believe the nature of the text supports such interjections, but wanted to make a note of it.

Another difficulty was the long string of idiomatic phrases in the final third of the text, and the even longer string of punning acronyms that follows. Where the Greek is too idiomatic for direct translation, I have substituted English equivalents, or at least phrases that explore the same subject. The acronyms that are broken down into phrases we discussed with the writer, and she felt the meaning of the phrase was more important than the meaning of the acronym word. I have managed to find tolerable English substitutes for most of the words, keeping the meaning of the Greek phrase. In some cases, the joke of the acronym had to be changed to preserve the resulting phrase, the most radical change being S.T.I.C.K. (Sever The Inimical Cord, Kiddo), which in Greek was K.T.E.Λ., a pun on the bus company. It was a stretch in Greek too, and I think the substitution works very well, preserving much of the meaning (Κόψε Τελειωτικά Εμφύλιους Λώρους) and the subsequent jokes. Of course, the pun in the title is imperfect – My Advice Is Relax; Off Yourself, Life's Absurd should properly be M.A.I.R.O.Y.L.A., but even though U and Y are the same letter in Greek, I couldn't quite bring myself to do it. Informal written English does use U for You, and that will have to do.

With the acronyms that are simply listed, I have taken some liberties, substituting letter strings more familiar to the English ear, so that E.Υ.Δ.A.Π., Δ.E.H., E.O.K., E.E., O.E., A.E., Π.A.E., becomes I.M.F., P.S.I., E.E.U., E.U., C.O.D., W.Y.S.I.W.Y.G., S.N.A.F.U., in a nod to more recent events. Again, I find this translation choice defensible, particularly as English does not share Greek's enthusiasm for acronyms, but wish to underline that the anachronistic political edge is absent in the original.

Please note also that the references to hell and devils in the final section of the play are not present in the original, but a translator's decision to foreshadow the revelation at the end by invoking associated language.

In 2013, Lancaster-based theatre company Sturgeon's Law staged *M.A.I.R.O.U.L.A.* in English for the first time. Directed by Stella Duffy, designed by Nerissa Cargill Thompson, and produced by Leo Burtin and performed by Aliki Chapple.

The woman in the kitchen of her apartment.

I'm not really myself. Not for a while now. I'm depressed, in a way, but not in the way most people get depressed. No pills and stuff and doctors, none of that. Not that fashionable, banal depression that you pay for hand over fist, spending your precious euros on it every week, no, I've got my own kind of depression, with which you can fuck perfectly normally, you can work, you're into going out, you can laugh, you can do everything, and not only can you do it but you take pleasure in it, it's just that to all of these activities you always bring the same attitude, the same philosophy, let's call it a contemporary school of philosophical thought, of your own invention, which says neither more nor less than, folks, this watermelon is a bit bleah, kind of bleah this watermelon, I mean we've cut it open and it's a bit pink, a bit unripe, not very juicy, but all the same we'll eat it with a good appetite, because we really wanted some watermelon like crazy but unfortunately it was a bit bleah. And unfortunately it was the only one we could find. In the whole market all that was left was this solitary watermelon which is perfectly fine, it cools you off, it quenches your thirst, it gives you the sense of having eaten watermelon, it's not a potato or anything, not a tomato, only just a bit bleah.

Stavros will be along soon to fuck me, he's a good fuck and we get along well, so at least I'm spared the sense of emptiness after this relatively indifferent fuck, 'cause we'll always have a laugh together afterwards, talk, play a game, and this affection between us gives me at least a feeling of tenderness and maybe that's why this relationship has lasted about a year, even though it's not love or anything. It's just a crutch, it's what I've always despised my whole life, the whole 'it's better than nothing' approach, which really used to turn me off as an attitude to life, well, here we are, I've come to appreciate it and worst of all, even to need it. I've arrived at this very unpleasant state, which is probably a part of the natural evolution of every human existence that paces with steady step ever closer to death, where I now wish for health, health above everything, where if I write in a birthday card I don't wish people a long life anymore, I don't write 'live many years' [that's what we say in Greek for "Happy Birthday", *Hronia Polla*, which means "may you live many years"] but "good years, good, that's the main thing", and other things like that, things that suck, and these are like all other things that suck, or at least like the two most popular things you suck, both of which we call pipes in Greek, *pipes*[1], the *pipa* you smoke, and the *pipa* where you suck a guy's cock, and here I want to add this thought which only just occurred to me, that it's no accident that we say things that are a bit bleah suck, that in Greek we call them *pipes*, it's not accidental at all, because both *pipes*, the smoking one as much as the cock one, they have a degree of mediocrity in common, I think any of us would be irritated by someone lighting up a pipe next to us, very few people actually like the smell of pipe smoke, and it's the same with sucking cock, this too, unless it's a case of passionate, blind love, usually, it's an act without much substance, without surprises, which is why when people ask 'Hey, whatever happened with that guy, did you two fuck or what?' you answer with an indifferent expression. 'Nah, nothing much, just a few blow jobs.' Well, I think that says it all.

So, awaiting the arrival of Stavros, lying on my couch, I make my hand into a pistol by raising my thumb vertically and pointing my index finger straight forward, hoping to kill my time (or one of the woodcocks[2] that you find here in Gazi, [that's my neighbourhood]) but unconsciously I bring my finger to my temple, and I think how everything's in vain and how bored I am of this apartment and how it's all in vain having an apartment, and how the whole satisfaction of holding a bunch of keys in your hand, with little hanging dolls and miniature shoes and other *pipes* like that, whose only purpose is to open a door, and not even a metaphorical door, the door of life, door of hope, or the door of dreams, but a plain wooden apartment door, and what's the point of that picture on the

[1] This is pronounced more like 'peeper' than 'piper'.

[2] It seems odd to find woodcocks in the centre of Athens. This may be a joke, though there is no rude connotation in Greek, or it may be used generically.

wall and what's the point of the photo of my parents and what's the point of all these books on the shelves that I read with so much passion once? What did they all teach me?

What did Euripides and Sophocles teach me in the end? Where did all these splendid people get me, all these great ideas and lofty sentiments, what did they have to offer beyond that moment where they moved me deeply? Nothing. So, what was the point, in the end? To move me? To make me cry over the fate of all flesh, and so over my own fate? Thank you very much, I was deeply moved, I don't want any more, though – I won't have more, thanks. So, now, what else can I do? Have you got anything else to offer, or was that it? Have you got anything else, besides useless knowledge, or do we just keep singing the same old song 'til the end, the whole cyclical nature of everything? This whole concept, this birth-death, happy-sad, black-white business, is it going to go on much longer, this process of subtraction, what I'm asking is, this postmodern one tiny dot on a white background where the painter spent his whole life painting realistically in order to finally arrive at that dot and the dot is considered to be a depiction of society and the incredible maturity of this painter, that at sixty he's painted a dot that says it all, and no longer needs brooks or bridges, portraits, tits, trees, this whole project of being born and dying alone, and I don't mean alone 'deserted' but alone with your just deserts, is it going to be in fashion long? Is it a bit like jeans, which will never go out of fashion? Because if that's how it is wall of mine, and picture, and curtain of mine, please tell me, so I'm not just sitting here pointlessly looking at you, and if, darling furniture, you're not going to find your voices and speak to me, at least give me a sign, something, Morse code, something to indicate the end of hope, we're closed, the security shutters are down, don't fret yourself dollbabie, fuck Stavros, cross yourself [and thank God] that you found a Stavros to cross your ankles behind, go out for a walk, see some friends, go on a little holiday, and it's over, that's it, there's nothing more. Bang. My finger pistol fires an invisible bullet into my brain. And why should there be anything more? Other people don't have even that. There are people who have no legs, who have nothing at all below the waist. Bang. Okay you cunts. I'll say thank you, too. All right.

I don't know if this condition of mine is subject to improvement, and I'm very much afraid it doesn't even have a course to run, not even downhill, not even to rock bottom, sacred rock bottom, that holy place that many years ago, in my foolishness I hated and was sick of, and hoped never to reach again, but now that I'm on my way to tedious wisdom, now that it's too late, now I can understand its true worth, o rock bottom, my darling rock bottom that at least drove me to extremes, made me fall blindly in love, scream on Skoufá Street, humiliate myself in front of strangers, drag myself around flat drunk on many a New Year's Eve over some unrequited love or another, broken bottles in my wake, o darling misery, where are you, and even more beloved cause of my misery, come back, rough seas of my youth, bring some change to this flat calm of maturity and gratitude for every tiny little ant I see before me, for every ray of sunlight, and every fucking day that dawns, send me someone I can call an asshole, take from me the knowledge that no-one is to blame for the way they are, take these doldrums from my spirit, take the compassion from my condescending little smile, take Jung and [Irvin] Yallom, take this bestseller they call balance, take this filthy film of positive energy, take the beautiful sunsets, and your organic products and stick them up your ass, please, shove them right up your ass, and give me back a reason to paint a bomb on the wall, give me cause to write FUCK YOU ALL in black marker on my desk, leave me to my narcissistic funk and not my artistic ability, o funk, where are you? How can I feel you, funk, when I'm waiting for Stavros, dear old Stavros, that good fellow who's alright with himself, that good fuck, that open-minded and well-educated fuck, who does everything well and whom I can't fault in anything? How? I'm screaming, and my posture is completely relaxed, I'm screaming when I'm sitting on the couch scratching my pubes, I'm screaming when I'm incredibly sleepy, I'm screaming on the inside and on the outside I'm yawning, I'm sick of myself, then again not completely, I'm a little bit sick of myself, I feel a bit okay, things are a bit alright, my life seems a bit balls, most people are a bit jerk-offs, our country's a bit of a toss-off, but not completely because of the good weather and the islands, and because no place is perfect, the work I've got to do this year I like a bit, I don't like myself much, but sometimes I do, and overall, this whole Checkhovian mediocrity of a mediocre human being is busting my balls a bit, but then again not completely, because I also find it moving, I like the truth of this sort-of-blahness and in the end I think I sort of like it that I realize, I mean I prefer it to me being a complete idiot and thinking everything was great, so I can't see much of a future for myself, and I don't much like that idea. I don't much like this discount store display of answers to the question 'How are you?' Okay man, sort of well, plugging away, it's going, well enough, can't complain, health, so long as we have our heath all other things can be managed. Of course we need our health, health is a wonderful thing, but I don't know about other things being managed, 'can't complain' isn't really gratitude, and humility, that's just plain stupid, and maybe in the end that's the real reason for the survival of the human race, not the instinct to reproduce, not the instinct to survive, but the simple stupidity of the species, the stupidity of the arrogance of believing that everything is in our power. And our folk culture, in its wisdom, our [Greek] tradition with all its wise proverbs never explains what these manageable things are. All other things, it says, can be managed [so long as we have our health]. Which other things? What things? These things or those things? Wait up, folks, whoah folks, first of all are you sure that your things are the same as my things and if everything is manageable, what are you complaining about? And I'm addressing this to you, who have your health and all your limbs and aren't suffering from any illness, what are you moaning about? Why are your songs so weepy, why is your poetry all about pain, why from the dawn of time up to the present day have you been calling on the gods to come down and save you, why all the alas and alack, you liars, what's manageable? I believe that if anything can be managed, that thing is health, that's all scientific progress can cure, I believe that physical health can, in some cases, perhaps be improved, but all the other possible things, never.

So, on impulse and in full cognizance of my own responsibility, I'm going to take the initiative and at this very moment, in a world first, I'm going to change the proverb, in my all-pervasive arrogance and pretentiousness, I'm going to change it and say 'So long as we don't have our health, some things might be managed'. And another thing. For people on their last legs, for the very, very, old, have you seen some old women on the street, you've seen them, who walk like this? Whose bodies are completely at right angles? For those people, who can only look down at fallen leaves and gobs of spit? Where's the proverb for them? For the very old person in a hospital bed, leaving this world, what saying is there? Is there a comforting proverb for them, or do we wish them too health, health above all? Of course not. So then, what do we do? Do we, in these circumstances, throw the folk wisdom in the trash? So, dear folk, don't think you're as wise as all that, I'm the one who's wise because I can adapt your proverbs, I'm the one who's wise because I think your proverbs are a pile of crap, sheer ignorance, a form of fatalism, 'You could wear yourself out knocking on the deaf man's door', says your folk wisdom, and I'm thinking what a jerk you'd have to be for going to the deaf man's door in the first place, and what a jerk the deaf man is for having a door. Maybe we can put some windows next to the deaf man's door, for the noise? I take the initiative, here in my joyless apartment, me who's nobody, just someone waiting to get fucked, I'll change this proverb too and shout 'Never knock on the deaf man's door, don't even try, leave the deaf with the deaf, what business have you got knocking on his door anyway, leave the deaf man to his deafness, but whatever you do, don't knock 'til you wear yourself out' No way. It's like telling you to spend your life trying to change something that can't be changed, this dangerous and anything but wise folk culture imposes this on you, to waste your time pleading outside the deaf man's house and the steam's coming out of your ears because he won't open his fucking door.

The doorbell rings and from this point on continues intermittently ringing.

That's Stavros, but because this is a solo show, as I'm sure you understand, we can't actually show you another character, and anyway, I'll just go into my bedroom for a while, that's where the scene with Stavros will take place, I don't think it'll take too long, Stavros, he's got to go to work afterwards, so I'll just go do what we're going to do and I'll be right back, I'll condense time a bit too, I mean it won't take as long as a real fuck, it'll be in theatre time, so relax, there'll be a short intermission while I'm gone, you'll wait for me to get back, I'll be back sometime, goodbye, so long, I'm going to get fucked, bye, I hope you're having a good time so far, don't feel jealous of me now when I go in, envy is a terrible thing and I'm being honest here it's not worth it, there's nothing to be jealous of really, if I were in your shoes I wouldn't envy me, I mean you'll see when I tell you about it afterwards, it's a very ordinary sort of fuck, the only possible reason for you to see it is so you'll feel lucky you're not in my place, just that and I don't mean the act itself, okay the act is roughly more or less the same whoever is doing it, it's not that, it's the expression on my face, my expression at the time is the saddest thing, especially when I'm on all fours and he can't see, that's where the gist of it is, I have this expression on my face, how to explain it, as if I were let's say an old shepherd who's spent his whole life up in the mountains and suddenly they stick a computer in front of me and say, hey old-timer, why don't you send an email, this, this, I don't know how to describe it, but at the same time I'm wearing that expression, my vocal chords are fully participating in the fuck, it's tragic, tragic, since I can't do it right now to show you, it's a bit, well, let's say I've taken my clothes off, I'm in the position, the expression on my face is about like this, and my voice like this, oh, oh, oh, oh, it's tragic, not getting what you want, tragic, it's like your organs don't belong to the same body, you are eyes, nose, ass, legs, breath, all separate, for you I hope that all your organs stay connected and dependant on each other, that your eyes don't head down let's say Patission Avenue while your mind is on Koumoundourou Square and you don't know where to take your feet, one foot here and the other there, I hope you never get your personality doing the splits, because it hurts, the fucker hurts, and especially I think in Greece, where we're not known for our rhythmic gymnastics, we're not the favourites to win a medal in those individual group routines, whatchamacall them

I don't want you to be affected by my condition, honestly I don't, because I know I'm only seeing one aspect of reality, here where I find myself, I see one aspect, and I don't want to impose anything on anyone, for some other people things are different, they're good, they are, and of course that's valid, there are things, the average life span has increased, there are a lot, there's creativity, there are the small pleasures of daily life, the surprises, the day spreading out before you, all yours, going for a walk on a sunny day, or another, a grey, rainy day and you're holed up snug in a coffee shop chatting away with your best friend, and you don't have work, there's nothing you've got to do, and the day is yours, all yours for strolling around the markets, buying some little thing for yourself, something nice, plans for next month, taking a trip somewhere, the prospect of it, unexpectedly meeting people, the seasons, pomegranates, the way you open them and all the seeds are all lined up next to each other in harmony, so perfect, there is so much, so much, there is, these things exist it's true, there are beautiful fabrics, wonderful evenings out in public squares, with trees, smells, cats sunning themselves contentedly in alleyways, people who've been together for years holding hands and window shopping, dogs who get lost and then find their people again, songs, their choruses, choruses.

So many choruses. How very many. And verses. Verses, but choruses too. And the verse is good, and choruses too because they lead to the next verse, you're like this and you're like that, I'm unhappy, what's happening to me, I'm a mess, the night is dark, and here comes the chorus, but in spite of it all I love you, good times will come again, and it saves it, saves it, that chorus saves it, no, it does, even the smallest thing has its meaning and its value, you just need to be there to see it, there are little things, there are, there are some very nice brassieres for them, for those who've had mastectomies, very nice, with a top on you can't tell at all, not at all, there are so

many, there are, things to take pleasure in, there are, there are
some beautiful cemeteries in some little villages, that you see
sometimes and you think, oh how wonderful to be buried here,
how wonderful, on this hillside, there's fresh air, this would be
a nice place for the years to go pleasantly by, very pleasantly,
you'd barely notice them going by, so nice, so my wish for you
is, what shall I wish for you, first of all that you have children,
those of you who don't, many children, many children to run
around smeared with jam and chocolate spread, all around
your built-in kitchen, and all around your IKEA house, and
don't you want any more IKEA, don't you like it? Stop going
there, never go there, shop somewhere else, let's abolish IKEA
and have another store like IKEA, AEKI, or KEAI, or AIAKI,
it can be called KEIA, whatever you want, I wish your children
all the best, may they grow up to be the people you dream
of, may they marry the person you dream of for them, how
to put it, the best, the best person, the best person in the
world, that one, that's who I hope your children marry, all of
your children, to marry that one person, the best person, all
children, that one person, may your children be lucky, joyful,
happy, may they laugh, have good teeth, straight teeth and a
nice smile, may they never get sick, never, may they never be
unhappy, no sadness, no pain, pain? Let it not exist at all, not
even the word, let the word mean something else, like, I don't
know, pane as in pane of glass[3], windowpane, that will be the
only kind of pane, so I hope your children never know loss,
at all, nor yourselves, especially yourselves, be well, because
if you're not well no-one will be well, not your children, not
the people around you, no-one will be well if you're not well,
be careful, because if you're not well then alas and alack, and
alas and alack, I don't know what you can do, take pills, find a
good therapist, get a pick-axe and pick, pick away at all your
Oedipal complexes, hunt, dig, scratch at your scars, you've

[3] The original joke here is based on the Greek word for pain, ponos,
being broken down to p-onos, (π – όνο), a convoluted pun involving
an archaic word for donkey and a zimmer frame or walker, called π
for its shape. It was simply not possible to translate in its original
form, and if anything, the pun works rather better in English.

got time, ooh, before you die, ooh lots of time, smoke a lot, take coke, go ahead, these things aren't dangerous, if you know how to handle them they're not dangerous, go ahead, it's never too late, do everything so long as you're well, live well so you can die satisfied, happy, calmly and beautifully extinguished with no pain, no illness, no desires left unfulfilled, you can, people can do anything if they put their minds to it, if they really want to, people find a way, there are thousands of ways, so many ways.

Ten ways to have an orgasm. Ten ways to make him love you. Ten ways to make your cock bigger. One hundred thousand ways to make your cock smaller. Four steps to happiness. One step closer to the edge. Families and magazines demonstrating the best way to live. The only way to live. How to manage on your own. In how many steps. You can on your own. Alone. Not needing anybody. You can stand on your own two feet. But my knees are bending. Stand up. But I'm bending. It doesn't matter. On all fours. I'm on all fours now. I'm walking on my knees, like a pilgrimage, the kind I've always made fun of, I'm making a pilgrimage too, on my knees, towards the monument of freedom. They can keep their blessed virgin of Tinos, and all that crap. To the monument of freedom. I've made it. I can manage on my own. I can manage all on my own. I can too, just like the Statue of Liberty. Alone, on my rocky little island. Vibrator in hand. Not in New York. No. Somewhere in the Aegean. It doesn't matter though. It's the same. Dildo in hand.

Varvara's got cancer. Alright. How old is she. Sixty. Sixty something. Eh, alright. Me, these days I get tired just walking up the stairs. Eh, alright. Alright, it's natural. My mother's getting old. Eh, alright. I haven't fallen in love for years. Alright. I eat genetically modified chicken. Alright, we all do. They grow the chickens without heads. Alright, the way things are now, that's natural too. Really? And what if it was your kid, growing up without a head? Alright, if that's how all other kids were too, alright. Who's going to tell Varvara about the cancer? Alright, we'll see. The loggerhead sea turtle is going

extinct. I don't give a shit. About the loggerhead sea turtle.
But the planet is being destroyed. Good. Good. I'll sit on my
couch and wait. For an earthquake I hope never ends. I won't
take shelter under the doorframe or the table. Here on the
couch. I'll use the controls on my TV remote to go up the
Richter scale. Six point one, six point two, six point three, six
point four, six point five, seven, eight, nine. Balls to the journey
to Ithaca. Blue. Hey, I want to get off. I get seasick on ferry
boats. I want to get off. This crossing, Piraeus to Ithaca, it's a
rough one. Very rough. I do understand that we're on the way
to Ithaca, I understand it well, and I like everybody on board,
even the stowaways, I just want to get off the boat, it's very
rough and I can't stand rough seas, I get dizzy, I puke, and I
don't want any more polite smiling well-meaning generous
crew members with nametags on their lapels that say Piraeus-
Ithaca giving me paper seasickness bags with a map of Ithaca
printed on them, I don't want them, I want to get off the boat.
And even though there's everything, there's First Class if you
want, there's a restaurant, and a nice view, and seagulls, and a
cabin, and a nice little shop, and cappuccino and fredoccino,
and latte and machiato and macchiatino and ciapattini and
pannini and panacottini and ciocholattofreddoccinato, and
everything but me, I'm feeling seasick.

The bell continues to ring.

And that's not really Stavros ringing the bell. The person
ringing the bell is the technician who's ringing the bell.
And behind my living room there's nothing. Nothing. A blank.
I'm in the void. I'm in a hot air balloon living room, I'm in a
living room floating in the void. I don't have neighbours.
I don't say good morning to the friendly head of the residents'
association. I don't pay fees for the cleaning the stairs and
fixing the elevator[4], I don't have an entrance. I don't know how
I got in here. I'm flying. This box I'm in is flying and I'm sitting
here watching TV until I get sleepy. I'm flying in my living room

---

[4] 'I don't pay fees for cleaning the stairs and fixing the elevator' is
a substitution for the Greek word koinohrista, meaning the fees
residents pay for the upkeep of the common areas in a block of flats.

over all the public squares, over all the beaches I've ever gone swimming, I'm flying and through the peephole in the front door I can see my first ever cigarette butt. I stubbed it out, stepping on it with my little girl shoe, I'm flying and through the peephole in the front door I can see my father, not pizza delivery guys with their motorbike helmets in hand, my father with no helmet, my father with that malignant star pinned to his brain, and the leaflets under my door aren't for pizza or souvlaki deliveries, nothing like that, they're announcements for funerals, memorial services, beloved sister, brother, mother, grandfather, today again we're interring our beloved. My beloved love affair. Today I'm re-burying. LOVE in capital letters. I turned the E around to make Poseidon's trident. Now I write it in lower case, and [in Greek] a lower case e looks like an ass.

Because the fuses in my house are always blowing, they blow if you turn a lot of things on at once. If you make the mistake of turning yourself on all at once. It gets dark. I buy little gas canisters from the supermarket so I can make coffee, extra canisters, just in case. In case I run out of gas someday and what will I do without coffee. My coffee commits suicide every day, gasses itself on the flames. I make Greek coffee in a *briki*[5] and the froth puffs up as it boils, swelling up like a boil and each bubble in the froth pops like a dream. And I'm afraid I won't turn the flame down in time and it'll boil over. I cut my dreams short so I'll be in time. So they won't boil over. It would be a shame to get scalded by boiling dreams. Better a coffee burn. I'll put toothpaste on my hand. If I have to. Where it hurts. And it'll still hurt but I'll bite my lip, because I'm too old to cry over things like that. I've grown up, matured. And maturity means self-harm with your own teeth, which are maybe even capped. Maybe, I don't remember. I'd bite my lip and make ugly grimaces, but what do I care, since no-one would be watching me. And with my other hand, the unscalded hand, I'd make a finger revolver, like this, and kill

---

[5] Briki is the small, long-handled metal pot used for boiling finely-milled coffee grounds with water to make Greek coffee (aka Turkish coffee).

cowboys with that bullet sound you make when you're a kid, bang, bang[6], cowboys because I always liked the Indians best, always, they're the ones I loved in cowboy movies, they're the ones I was going to fuck when I got older, them, the long-haired guys who made a mess of everything, but in the end I grew up a bit and I went out with the sheriff, in the end I fucked the sheriff, and all my good blow job technique I gave to him in the end, because with him we went out to fancy restaurants and fashionable parties. And we got our pictures [in magazines]. And I liked it.

Cliché Greek hit, De Milame by Paschalis Terzis. She puts it on herself, on the CD player, dances to it, in the end she uses her top to cover part of her face, as if she's taking her top off.

I used my top as a mask, that was a bit of directorial inspiration. Good? Good, right. It was to give me something to do, to break the monotony, to underline the sentiment, to provoke a bit more attention, to highlight with that gesture the shape of my internal distress, my own heart's truth isn't enough for me, I want to sell it too, I want my airy nothing to be liked, to have aesthetic value, to be a tasteful bit of nothing, is the mask good? Good? Aaaaah.

Is it moving? Ouaaaah.

And all that just to feed my self-centredness, keep me in the spotlight a bit longer to say, hey, I'm here too, here, here, over here, hey, I'm suffering, pay attention to me, I'm going to die pay attention to me, I can't bear it anymore pay attention to me, all my noble sentiments are so people will say how good she is, all my rebellion is so people will say, wow that girl is really radical, I circulate my pain and my break-ups through the mobile phone network, oh, I'm not doing well, let's talk later, message sent, I've got a lot to tell you, send message now okay, I send my moaning by typing oh, aitch, oh, aitch, uttered without breath to some impersonal satellite, I admire

[6] bam, bam in Greek.

myself weeping over the mess that life is, but I give a bit of what I can spare to the guy cleaning windshields at the traffic light, the few coins scattered on the passenger seat, I offer him my compassion too so I'll be rewarded by the eyes of some nonexistent god within me, I offer, though I want to tell that guy who cleans my windshield whether I want him to or not, go fuck yourself, you're filthy. Fuck you and your country.

But if I'm in a good mood one day, I might give him a whole fiver, all of five euros to the filthy windshield guy, and so the immigrant prospers because some mother's son was inspired to text "you're so fucking hot" to my mobile, wild party time for the guys at the traffic lights, because my self-confidence is up a bit, then I can get all philanthropic and everything, so I can be the soul of charity or a monster, it's all the same, it depends on my mood, it depends on how many years it's been since I believed in something absolutely, the way I used to believe before that maturity I was talking about, depends on just how hard the loneliness is hitting me, depends on how much money I have to spend just then, depends on whether I had a good night's sleep. Oh, brother. No real faith or values, it all depends, and add contemporary psychotherapy into the mix, a new religion telling me that I've got issues with anger, anger, because something got disturbed, some pubic hair got in my DNA, because the third tooth on the left in the mouth of my grandmother's brother had high cholesterol, or because my mother's femininity was unsexed by the ambitions that my grandfather's false teeth harbored for her, and that I need to let that anger go.

To not be angry. Why should I let it go? Why? What's wrong with carrying your anger around? It's alright for people to carry their anger openly? Yes lady, it is. It's the fashion. This year, all shades of purple are in, and pink hair, and the affirmation of life. The new fashion is to kill whatever made me this way, the new fashion is to kill whoever gave me birth and whoever gave birth to whoever gave me birth and whoever was before the one who gave birth to whoever gave me birth, so to kill who, then? A dinosaur? A tyrannosaurus? An ape? Who exactly should I kill, what zoo should I go to, to find my ancestors and why? So I can become what? A new kind of person? A weed, that just grew without being planted? To be a monster, but a monster in good mental health? A healthy monster?

Did my message get sent? Was it sent? Because I've got another one. There are conditions and terms that aren't recognized by science, conditions not called hypochondria or agoraphobia or claustrophobia or nyphomania or panic attack or depression there are conditions like habit, like bad taste, like 'I've got a screw loose' like 'that's the cherry on the shit-cake', like 'I'm an ugly bastard but I still get laid because I have a bit of power and though I'm preening next to the sexiest piece of ass in the world, my face will always be the face of that fat kid at school who had zero success with babes' there's stinginess, and the scientific term for that is 'crabs in your pockets' there's 'meet the new boss, same as the old boss' and there's also 'we'll vanish off the face of the earth' there are illnesses like 'I'm pining away for love of you' or 'I am a rock, I am an island' or 'the fool returns to his folly' or 'you can't judge a book by its cover' and I want to know if there are pills for these conditions, is there a pill for 'give them an inch and they'll take a mile' isn't there one of these new advanced pills without the old side-effects? And I get a new message and I press okay and I read that I'm the one with a problem and I read that I need to find some balance, and I read that what's wrong with me is fedupness and that there are miracle pills for that, of course, there's everything for anything, and for fedupness there are dupny pills, which are from somewhere exotic, that's why they've got such a strange name, and they look like peanuts, they've got like a shell all around that you peel off and leave in the ashtray, and you take the pills, dupny pills, Du Puy pills they call them in France, no there's, there is, what there is there is, there's one to keep you on an even keel, so you don't get too many ups and downs and it's called 'Dancing', no, there's 'smileacrum' that's got two meanings, 'smileacrum' because it makes you want to smile even when things are crummy, it makes the corners of your lips turn up, like a crescent moon, like the moon the cow jumped over, a simulacrum of a smile, the names of medications really get to me, they're just marketing tricks by pharmaceutical companies, but D.A.N.C.I.N.G.? That's nice, appealing, better than calling it alaphrosyl for example, as soon as you hear that you feel mentally ill whether you are or not, but D.A.N.C.I.N.G. with its pretty little full stops, stands for Doctor Adieu, Now Cured I Nonchalantly Go. Or maybe you burst into tears and you cry, and cry, cry, cry. You're crying? Are you an idiot? What are you crying about? About nothing? Yes, exactly, that's what I'm crying about. Nothing. Well, don't. Here, take this. Take S.H.I.T., yes, just the way it sounds, S.H.I.T. stands for Sadness Halted Immediately: Today. Or, if you want a placid disposition and a gentle gaze, like a cow, there are other pills, pills with names like the cows in a dairy herd, Buttercup, Marigold, Daisy. D.A.I.S.Y. for example means Doctors Are Incompetent Save Yourself, there's U.N.E.S.C.O., Unfortunately No-one Escapes, Second Chances Over, U.N.E.S.C.O., so, that means Second Chances Over, C O, let's see, there's C.O.–O.P. Certainly Over–Optimistic, Princess. I.C.B.M., It's Crap, Believe Me. I.C.B.M., Codswallop, Believe Me. I.C.B.M.B.M., O.P.E.C., O.T.E. still stands for the Telecommunications Organization of Greece, they left that one alone, don't ask me why, there's F.A.R.T.I.N.G., which makes you fart. That. That's what they prescribe for love, when you've got a dangerous case, Farting Around Ruining Things Instead Of Making Them Noble & Great, it's got that OMT in the middle, and the 'and', so it's F.A.R.T.I.O.M.K.T.N&G., properly, but you can't go up and ask for some F.A.R.T.I.O.M.K.T.N&G. at the counter, so it's F.A.R.T.I.N.G. for short F.A.R.T.I.O.M.K.T.N&G., I.M.F, P.S.I., E.E.U., E.U., C.O.D., W.Y.S.I.W.Y.G., S.N.A.F.U., T.E.S.T.I.C.L.E.S., Therefore, Enquire: Should Tenderness Incapacitate Critical Life Enhancing Systems? T.E.S.T.I.C.L.E.S., T.E.S., T.E.S., Tee Ee Ess, Truly Entertaining Silliness? T.I.C.L.E.S. To Instigate Collective Loving Embrace Sweetly Is What Happiness Needs. W.H.N. What Happiness Needs? Testicles is what happiness needs. Happiness requires balls. The pill is called I.W.H.N. and anything you swallow is a pill, anything with full stops is a pill, I swallow those little dots from 1 to 1,000 and inside my guts I join them all up with a ballpoint pen to make the picture appear, me wearing swimming flippers, me smoking a cigarette, me sunbathing, me on the sun-lounger on my little Cycladic island, me with my legs open, waiting, there's a magic image, not waiting for the gynecologist, nor for anyone's cock, nor for the bald head of a baby to emerge, with my legs open waiting for the hot water, magic. So I can take a bath. Magic. So I can go out for a drink. Magic.

There's also a pill called S.T.I.C.K., just the way it sounds, S.T.I.C.K., because isn't a stick a kind of root? Going back to your roots, like taking the bus back home to your village for the summer? Well, because modern psychotherapy's all about blaming your family, they've brought out S.T.I.C.K., which stands for Sever The Inimical Cord, Kiddo. Now, properly, it should be called S.T.U.C.K. Sever The Umbilical Cord, Kiddo, but you don't want to give people the impression they're going to stay stuck, and it was a shame to ruin the acronym, 'cause it's a good idea, you wouldn't want to throw it out for one word, so they made umbilical cord into inimical cord which, it goes without saying, I think is better, more poetic, much better, and it conveys the substance better: Inimical cord. That civil war you always find yourself fighting against your own flesh and blood, right? Against your mother and your father, the source of all ills. Your miserable parents whose likeness you spend your life trying to find in a romantic partner, and you're always disappointed, and you suffer, because you fell in love with the wrong person, wrong, wrong, because you're never going to find your daddy, girl, that's what psychology tells us, stop looking for him in yet another guy, that Takis, that Vangelakis, that Stavrakis, girl, he is not your daddy. So what do you know, psychologist, maybe I'm cool with looking for daddy, why is it any better looking for the milkman, who died and made you the authority on what is or isn't good for people's psychological wellbeing? And don't feed me that pap about freedom and independence, not while with the other hand you're imposing your petty-bourgeois morality on me, the new threefold drug that every happy loser's addicted to, work, family, creativity. The end, perfect, that's all. So finally, how many sessions do I need, or rather how many euros will it take to make me want to stop wanting to blow daddy, how many euros do I have to give you before I'm happy to be alive and getting old and that my chest hurts from all the cigarettes I've smoked, and that can I run riot in Exarheia, screaming like a 15-year old and that same night lie in bed squeezing my tits in case one of them's got a lump in it like a ping-pong ball.

And then there is the one and only miracle pill, I saved it for last, this is the miracle pill. M.A.I.R.O.U.L.A. Mairoula is in a box, just one pill per box, because you only take it once and that's that. It's a pill you only take once and all your problems are over. M.A.I.R.O.U.L.A. stands for My Advice Is Relax; Off Yourself, Life's Absurd. That's this pill right here. Mairoula.

Which I'm going to take, tonight, here, in front of everybody, not because there aren't good things in the world, not that, there are, there are all kinds of good things, there's shoe soles, the non-slip kind for walking on ice, you can get them on boots, really good boot soles, very nice, no there are, there are many things, many good things, but me I'm going to take this pill, because, just because, because no cause, because I said so, because, because, cause be. So there.

At this point I'd like to thank the theatre, as a building, and as an idea, and as a profession, I'd like to thank punctuation marks and especially question marks for their kind contribution to my life, and I'd like to thank the Greek tomato for the memory of its flavour which still gives me goose-bumps and for its gradual adulteration, which provides so many opportunities to communicate with my fellow human beings by repeating the phrase 'hey, whatever happened to tomatoes?' 'hey, whatever happened to tomatoes?'

Takes the pill.

I've been told it takes about five minutes to kick in.

You don't have to wait with me.

I'm done. You can go. Or stay. As you like. Good-bye. I'm dying.

At this point, the actor is free to improvise whatever, lying on the kitchen table and addressing the audience. She could tell a joke she never gets to the punch line of, or begin announcing something important and die before she gets to it. When we did it at the National Theatre of Greece, we chose for her to start revealing a salacious bit of gossip about the Artistic Director and die before she got to the meat of it.

Dies.

In the afterlife.

Having wings and being unable to fly, it's incongruous, incomprehensible, it's entirely Greek, it's thinking like a chicken, trying to take flight and falling flat, and trying again, again and again falling flat on your face, the way that song about seagulls flying among the masts of ships[7] can only bring tears to your eyes, that illusion that you might even be a bird, a moment's delight, then the disappointment of falling flat every time you try. I was buried, with all the appropriate tears and Stavros had a front-row seat, he was even a pallbearer, sobbing broken-hearted, I couldn't even go 'na'[8], not just because he wouldn't be able to see me, but also because it's cramped inside a coffin, the gesture just isn't possible, there, 'na', 'na', trapped, and the crap they were saying about me was unbelievable, the reasons why I killed myself, that I had a thing about it, that I was eccentric, that's the kind of person who commits suicide, my kind of person that is, the kind who's never mentioned suicide, my kind of person, oh, the balls my poor ears heard uttered, and not a word to the point, from anybody. I saw all sorts of people, but the one who cried most was my cousin Pavlos. I hadn't even expected him to turn up. He was with his wife. And the toupée, o people, the toupée, why do they even wear them, they're so obvious, I don't get it, I really don't, and

---

[7] Oi Glaroi, 1966, (The Seagulls) Music by Nikos Meimaris, lyrics by Haralambos Vasiliadis.

[8] The Greek word is the exclamation that goes with an open-palmed gesture of scorn, a bit like throwing a snowball. She's retrospectively 'giving the palm'.

because he was crying so much, it kept slipping off, in the end it was all on the right-hand side of his head, stuck to his cheek, and poor Varvara went and straightened it for him. I was really impressed though, because we hadn't spoken in years, what do I mean 'spoken'? We've never spoken. They're deaf-mutes. Him and his wife. How could we speak? When we were kids in Larissa, we used gestures. Then I came to Athens and we lost touch, we couldn't even speak on the phone. What can you say on the phone? Ghghh and mmmm. Even with gestures, me and Pavlos, it was hit and miss. I'd go like this 'you're a jerk-off' and he'd go bring me the dice, thinking I wanted to play board games. He's an idiot too, anyway, I shouldn't be mean about him, the guy's got a disability, and he came to my funeral and everything.

So I'm in my coffin, you see, and it's sheer torture, on my back, [with the wings all crammed in there], there's even a feather going up my ass, awful, and my soul trying to fly away and not finding a way out, in the end it just stayed, stayed with me, even my soul went for the devil it knows, even my soul got tired of trying, and I was pushing it, go you fucker, go waft above their heads, go, you'll get eaten by worms down here, go, jerk-off, let's do our bit for Christianity and the eternal soul, she's not budging, what do you mean Christianity, now we're going to start giving a shit about Christianity, back in my body she goes, and after the party's over, after everybody's gone home to live their lives and remember me, because that's what it comes to, living to be remembered, well, we set off and I'll tell you this, I wasn't expecting it but being dead is something you experience, you live through your death and it's all true, all the stuff we talk about and laugh, like in a cartoon by Arkas[9], it's all true, St. Peter and everything, with a white beard, but not nice, not a sweetie-pie like in the stories, but a bit mean and neurotic and very conservative, not at all like the kindly old guy you expect, nicotine yellow teeth, thin-lipped with a

[9] Prolific and popular contemporary cartoonist who did a gag strip series about Heaven.

humpback, and really neurotic, a guy who's never satisfied,
who anticipates your arrival, the kind of guy who's got hold
of some power and knows that they can fuck you up if they
want to, the kind of guy who had god knows what done to
him when he was a kid and that's why he's the way he is, you
can't really blame him, but I see him there waiting for me, at
the gate, unfiltered cigarette in his mouth, and this little smile,
enough to make you sick, and short, oh my oh my, very short,
made me want to say so they've elevated you to sainthood,
hey shorty, and no sooner than I see him there at the gate,
I don't have time to say a word, nothing, fwap, he slaps me
right across the face, fwap, hard, and he starts aren't you
ashamed of yourself, have you no shame at all and fwap, slaps
me again, and again, and I fall down and he's grabbed me by
the hair, and he's shouting and spitting at me, and I'm covered
in spit, and on top of everything I'm grossed out, and it hurts,
suicide you sicko, suicide, and he's hitting me some more,
when there are people struggling so hard to survive, when
there are people whose kids die and still they soldier on, you
pervert, you filthy pervert, there are people dying of cancer
who still love life you idiot, people with cancer smiling you
stupid idiot, and as soon as I hear his accent I'm going, oh so
you're one us, Peter my boy, a country bumpkin like me, and
his eyes bug out, and you're making fun of me too, and on top
of it all you're making fun of me too, and more slapping 'til my
jaw's nearly dislocated, so the saint is a selfish jerk, the saint is
trouble, I can't stand people who take shit personally, I can't
stand them, but I wasn't going to let him win, noooo, it hurt,
it hurt like hell but I wasn't going to let him win, what is it, you
hick, I said, what is it you old goat, are you offended, I saw red
and fwap I hit him back, he doesn't scare me, I thought I'll fuck
you up six ways from Sunday, come by, come by, come by[10],
I keep at it, I'm almost fainting with the pain but, come by,
sheep, where's your flock of sheep Petey-boy, and fwap he's

---

[10] The Greek text here says 'derr derr derr' and 'prrrr'; sounds
a shepherd makes calling in sheep. 'Come by' is the only sheep
call I can find in English (British, not U.S), though it may be unfamiliar
to most readers.

still hitting me and with the last slap my chin's off to the right, the way my face went sideways with each slap and it came back, well this time it doesn't come back, my chin's still off to the right, dislocated jaw, bye-bye chin, it's gone, not coming back, eh, so I stopped there, I figure let it go 'cause shorty's lost it, and of course it hurts like fuck, serious pain, pain oh pain, I started crying, I'd had enough, my soul, my soul was frightened, he was going to kill me, he was choking me, he'd really lost it, and he wasn't wrong, the things he was saying, what could I say? I started to faint, I was losing consciousness, he grabs me by the throat in his rage, throws me to the floor and he's yelling, no shame at all and he's banging my head on the floor, bang, bang, bang, I was freaking out, and damned if Tsitsanis[11] doesn't turn up right then, like an angel, with his white wings and his voice deep and steady, hey let her go, he says, let her go, just like that, plain and simple, like a man, ballsy, if you'll excuse the impression, but a man, 'cause as soon as the other guy hears him, he lets me go, immediately, he lets me go but for a while afterwards its like his fingers are still clamped around my throat and I can't breathe, I'm coughing, coughing all curled up on the floor and just then, very gently, Tsitsanis standing next to me, Tsitsanis himself? So I'm lying there dying and Tsitsanis starts up next to me, dringi drang dran dran 'You won't turn and look at me/despise me as an enemy/have you forgotten that you wept over me/tell me why you've changed, why'[12] and I burst into tears, I'm crying not just because it's a beautiful song, not just that, but because it wasn't his song, the magnanimity of it, I mean look, a guy who's written hundreds of songs, thousands, and he chooses someone else's song to comfort me with, for me, there was that too, that it was for me, to comfort me, but with someone else's song, which means what? That he thinks it's better, or at least more suited to the circumstances, that's what made me

[11] Vassilis Tsitsanis (1915-1984), hugely popular songwriter and bouzouki player, one of the leading figures of Rebetika music.

[12] This, with the dringi-dran representing bouzouki music, is a famous old song Giati allaxes giati 1950 (Why have you changed, why?) by Kiromitis and Manesi.

cry. 'You won't turn and look at me/despise me as an enemy/ have you forgotten that you wept over me/tell me why you've changed, why' and with these words I think, what I've always thought really, I do feel comforted because other people have known loss, have felt the lack of someone, have lost someone, fine, but why is that comforting, what does it change about my loss, what, even if another ten million people have felt the same way, what does it change about the fact of loss, and at that moment I have a flash of realization and I say to myself, I was right to kill myself, I did fine, why should I sit here trying to patch up my soul with a needle and thread and crap like that, why should I fill up with holes and empty spaces just because that's how life is, why should I accept it, that that's how life is, and I start to feel very pleased with myself and ooop, I'm full of myself and aaaah, I feel a sort of aaaah.

So I'm feeling good about my insight, and just when I'm congratulating myself, telling myself how right I was, suddenly I'm on the flipside, hey what did I go and die for, me, when other people would pray to be as strong as I am, me who did so many things, who never did anybody any harm, me, who went on walks, whom nobody had an unkind word for, I went and did this idiotic thing, me that everybody was always so nice about, me with my talent and my beauty and everything, meeeee, and hup! Suddenly my self-confidence is up and I'm all, I'll fuck you all, I'll fuck you up, what do you mean I've got a thing and I'm eccentric, hey you, your ass is eccentric, hey Pete, hey, sainty-boy, hey god, beardie, get yourself over here, come here, I want to go back, hey I want to go back, hey you little cunt, I changed my mind, I repent, I can handle it now, it doesn't have to be a big deal, no big deal, nothing important, I don't want anything really, just to take a walk around Syntagma, check out the ceremonial guard, look around, nothing much, but saint hick is nowhere to be found, and the other guy next to me still with the dringi dringi dringi, there's a point at which dringi dringi in your ear gets to you, and I like Tsitsanis, and I'm honoured to have him all to myself, but couldn't he play some Tsitsanis? Imagine, having the one and only Tsitsanis playing for you, and he's not playing one of his big hits but some random dringi dringi? And I thought he was singing off key, of course I don't know much about music, but to my ear something was off, something was bothering me, eh so I get angry, it doesn't take much to set me off, and I grab him here, by the collar, and I say hey, why don't you say something too, they'll listen to you, don't torture me, put that thing down, you're making me dizzy, driving me crazy, hey, tell them to get me out of here, I'll go crazy in here, and while I've got him like that and I'm shaking him, my hand slips, like this, my hand goes this way, and I'm angry, it goes hrap, hits him here in the face, hrap, and his moustache comes off, the whole moustache, in my hand, I look at it, I look at it again, it wasn't really Tsitsanis, I'm frozen with shock, illusions here too, have they no shame, lies here too, con games in the afterlife everybody, con games up here, get lost, you're despicable, but what did I expect, it's the same people here, the same as down there, and I'm standing there like a fool with a false mustache in my hand, who the hell are you I say, hey who are you, what kind of game are you playing, where am I, I say, who are you, who are all of you, where's the short guy? He doesn't say anything, not a word. Go on, play Cloudy Sunday[13], not a peep from him, play Cloudy Sunday if you're a man, you liar, what the hell are you, are you a thief, what are you, here, take everything, take it all, and I open my bag, I'm beside myself, completely beside myself, here's me, over here's myself, that's what I'm talking about. He's looking at me. I'm going like this, like this. You're in Hell, lady, in Hell. I know I'm in fucking Hell, I tell him, I know, I know where I am, I know who I am and where I am. Who are you? Lady, he says, it's not just bad people who go to hell, it's also suicides, so lady, don't expect any saints here, no Tsitsanis, no Hatzidakis[14] no nothing. And who are you, I ask him, what are you, where are you from. Speak up!

---

[13] "Synefiasmeni Kyriaki" Tsitsanis's great hit and one of the most famous songs in Greece.

[14] Manos Hatzidakis (1925-1994), composer best known for pop songs and for theatrical and film music, including Never on Sunday, whose title song is a global shorthand for Greek music.

Karyotakis[15], he says. Karyotakis, and he gives me his hand like this. Karyotakis. And I give him my hand. And inside, I'm thinking, I get it, this is going to be fun, it's going to be a barrel of laughs up here, oh joy, what fun. And tsak, he grabs back the moustache, and tsak, he sticks it back on nice and secure like this here, grabs the bouzouki and starts with the dringi dringi dringi dringi dringi dringi dringi dringi and that's what happens here, all the time, dringi dringi, and it's going to keep happening, aaaaah, all the time, and so I don't go completely crazy with this Karyotakis character, I sit down next to him and go opa, opa, opa, opa[16], he's pleased, I'm clapping in time and opa opa and every now and then I throw in a 'health to you, Tsitsanis with your clever fingers' and he's pleased. What else can I do?

[15] Konstantinos Karyotakis (1896-1928) Modern Greek lyric poet and prose writer. He killed himself at the age of 32.

[16] This exclamation, roughly equivalent to the Spalish 'olé' denotes appreciation of skill and enjoyment of the moment.

Lena Kitsopoulou was born and lives in Athens. She is a graduate of Karolos Koun Drama School (1994). As an actress she has participated and participates in classic and modern plays, as well as in cinema. In 1997 she received the Best Actress award at Thessaloniki International Film Festival for the film *No Sympathy For the Devil* directed by Dimitris Athanitis.

In 2006 her first collection of short stories was released by Kedros publishing, under the title *Nichterides (Bats)* which received the Best Debut Author award in 2007. She has been working as a writer and a director ever since. She writes for newspapers and for collections of short stories, the most recent one being *Apotipomata tis Krisis (Crisis Impressions)*, 2013. In 2011 her second collection of short stories was released, *Megali Dromi (Great Roads)*.

She wrote and directed the *M.A.I.R.O.U.L.A.* monologue (2009), *Aoustras or the Hardness* (2011) for the National Theatre and *Athanasios Diakos – The Return* for the Athens Festival (2012). She directed *The Woman from Patras* by George Chronas (Apo Michanis Theatre, tour), and *Chere Nimphi (Greeting Nymph)* by Gregorios Xenopoulos (2011, Art Theatre). She directed and acted in the play *Ludus, Lucta, Illusio*, a narration of the novel by H. Kleist, *The Duel*, in collaboration with the early music ensemble and *Ex Silentio* (2013 Athens Festival). In February 2016 She directed Hedda Gabler, at Theater Oberhausen in Germany.

Her play *A day like any other day... the futility of living* (*Theatro Technis 2015*) was performed in December 2016 at Saint Gervais Theatre in Geneva. In October 2016, she presented her new play *Antigone – LONELY PLANET*, at Onassis Cultural Centre of New York, NY.

Her plays and texts are played by several playhouses in Greece and abroad. In Spring 2017, she will write and direct at the Experimental Stage of the National Theatre, a new play under the title *Tyrannosauri REX*.

In 2012 she participated in two one act plays, *N-eurose* and *The Price*, in two European Theatre Festivals, Wake – up, Voicing Resistance in Berlin and Theatre Uncut in London. Her plays have been translated in English, French, German, Spanish and Polish. For her play *Athanasios Diakos – The Return* she received the National Playwright award (Interanationaler Autorenpreis) in Heidelberg, during the 2013 Heidelberger Stückemarkt.

In May 2014 her play *Red Riding Hood – the First Blood* was presented in Onassis Cultural Centre, under her direction and at Theatre de la Ville in Paris. It was also presented as a staged reading at the Saint Gervais theatre in Geneva.

ANGELSTATE
by Nina Rapi

Translated by Nina Rapi

docile bodies...

Suppression and Desire in Nina Rapi's Angelstate

Nina Rapi belongs to a new generation of Greek dramatists, which defends a more politically aware theatre profoundly uninterested in the traditionalist dramatic forms and ideologies. One of the prominent features of this new dramaturgy is the rejection of the so-called "theatre of everyday life"[1] and the micro-problems of daily living, which often adopted a very uncritical stance towards Modern Greek conservatism. Instead of limiting the plays to localized microcosms, many contemporary playwrights have chosen to de-familiarize events, not simply in the Brechtian sense of making them strange[2], but by expanding situations into paradigmatic dramaturgical conditions which function as dramaturgical diagrams/patterns of living in a hostile and unfamiliar world (most often by removing time, place and social frame), sending thereby a universal message for the need of reconstructing the dominant structures of normality. Heavily influenced by contemporary British theatre, Nina Rapi follows the example of those playwrights, like Martin Crimp or Caryl Churchill, who defy "set norms and typical expectations for dramatic discourse in order to arrive at an unprecedented level of potentiality and signification"[3].

Angelstate is a study on the social suppression of desire and the distribution of discipline. In an imaginary space of expiation,

---

[1] Platon Mavromoustakos, *Το θέατρο στην Ελλάδα 1940-2000. Μια επισκόπηση*, The Theatre in Greece 1940-2000. An Overview, Kastaniotis, Athens 2005, p. 114

[2] De-familiarization was for Bertolt Brecht ("Notes to *Die Rundköpfe und die Spitzköpfe* (Description of the Copenhagen production)", in John Willett (ed.), Brecht on Theatre, (trans.) J. Willett, Methuen, London 1964, (pp. 100-103), p. 101), the basic tool for critically distancing the spectator from the normally expected by "stripping the event of its self-evident, familiar, obvious quality"

[3] Vicky Angelaki, *Introduction*, in eadem (ed.), *Contemporary British Theatre: Breaking New Ground*, Parlgrave Macmillan, Hampshire 2013, (pp. 1-8), p. 5

punishment and mainly self-punishment six characters under strict surveillance retrace their stories and their 'misdeeds', all related to the expression of a desire. It is not coincidental that the typology of the dramatic characters (Bodyguard, Bodybuilder, Anorexic, Dominatrix, the Priest) is related to the suppression or self-imposed control of desire, but it is also indicative of the characters' general deviation from the assumed canonical body. The abstract and stylized use of the expressionist "characterization" is intended to reflect social conditions and pathologies rather than actual everyday problems, and it deliberately exposes the artificiality or social typicality of the dramatic figures, making them paradigmatic in the human commonness of their suffering, but not unhistorical, in a very posthumanist[4] manner.

The condition within which the play's characters are placed, an angel-state, is a condition of being, dramaturgically transformed into an ambiguous liminal space of existential suspension, that is, a laboratory-prison cum Purgatory, where the characters of the play act confessionally under the watchful eye of the authorities which historically produce and control *docile bodies*[5]. As a result, the *dramatis personae* (if they can be called 'persons') become dramaturgical beings, reliving their inherent weaknesses and contradictions always in connection with a social rule, but way beyond any notion of everyday life. The angel-state is primarily a condition of self-realization, offering also the possibility of

---

[4] "The posthuman cannot simply be identified as a culture or age that comes 'after' the human, for the very idea of such a passage, however measured or qualified it may be, continues to rely upon a humanist narrative of historical change. [...] If, however, the posthuman truly involves a fundamental change or mutation in the concept of the human, this would seem to imply that history and culture cannot continue to be figured in reference to this concept", R. L. Rutsky, *Mutation, History, and Fantasy in the Posthuman, Subject Matters: A Journal of Communication and the Self*, 3.2/4.1, 2007, (pp. 99-112), p. 107

[5] Michel Foucault's infamous term in his *Discipline and Punish: The Birth of the Prison*, (trans.) Allen Lane, Penguin Press, London 1977, p. 135

expanding the personal limits of desire but only to those willing to switch into to a new personal structure of exoneration and refusal of guilt. Thus the play has a much broader Foucauldian focus and relevance, namely to adhere to "a genealogy of the present scientifico-legal complex from which the power to punish derives its bases, justifications, and rules" in order to portray how "a specific mode of subjection was able to give birth to man as an object of knowledge for a discourse with a scientific status"[6].

All the inmates of the *Angelstate* create a rupture in or even denounce the social canons under the normalizing gaze of state surveillance. They have all been engaged in a power relation within which they found themselves either in the position of perpetrator/giver, or victim/receiver. Along the same vein, they were all involved in a relationship of either giving, or receiving pain or even 'evil'. Namely, the Missionary's duty is to impose evil, the Body Builder is subjected to fatherly 'punishments' in the context of love, the Bodyguard accepts the loss of sexual love resolutely, the Priest deviates and is erotically drawn to someone beyond the morality of his conscience.

It is not coincidental that only the Dominatrix defends her actions until the very end: "And what does love mean? To want to give pleasure more than to receive it. This is love, I suppose". The sadistic subject, a representation of legitimate female imposition, is not only a stable form of female dominance, but also an allegory for social relations. Sadomasochism is after all a theatre of sexual desire, linked not only to pain itself, but to the eroticization of the desire for pain and pleasure in the sense of an erotic legitimization of (socially) forbidden forces:

> We choose the most terrifying, repulsive and unacceptable activities and we transform them into pleasure. We use all the forbidden symbols and all the denounced feelings [...]. The basic dynamic of Sadomasochism lies in the *dichotomy of power*, not in pain. The handcuffs, the dog

[6] Ibid., pp. 23-24

collars, the whips, the kneeling, the tying up [...] and serving somebody sexually – they are all metaphors [...]', which dramatize social inequality.

Finally, *Angelstate* is subversively queer, not because women in the play desire women, but mainly because it ventures to critically comment on the subject of female desire outside the centre of normality. The definition of 'queer' given by David Halperin is remarkably appropriate, precisely because 'queer' is:

> whatever is *at odds with the normal*, the legitimate, the dominant. 'Queer' then demarcates not a positivity, but a positionality *vis-a-vis* the normative. [...] Queer in any case, does not designate a class of already objectified pathologies or perversions; rather, it describes a horizon of possibilities whose precise extent and heterogeneous scope cannot in principle be delimited in advance. It is from this eccentric positionality occupied by the queer subject, that it may become possible to envision a variety of possibilities for *reordering* the relations among sexual behaviors, erotic identities, constructions of gender, *forms of knowledge, regimes of enunciation, logics of representation, modes of self-constitution* and practices of community.[8]

The regimes of enunciation are changing in contemporary Greek Theatre and *Angelstate* is a special verdict on power and desire in as much as it bears the power of performance, that is, "a more conceptually astute and inclusionary way of thinking about many subaltern cultural practices and intellectual-philosophical

[7] Pat Califia, *Unravelling the Sexual Fringe: A Secret Side of Lesbian Sexuality, The Advocate*, 27.12.1979, (pp. 19-22), p. 19, as cited in: Jeffrey Weeks, *The Meaning of Diversity*, Peter M. Nardi – Beth E. Schneider (eds.), *Social Perspectives in Lesbian and Gay Studies*, Routledge, London and New York 1998, (pp. 325-26), pp. 312-33

[8] David Halperin, *Saint Foucault: Towards a Gay Hagiography*, Oxford University Press, New York – Oxford 1995, p. 62

activities"[9]. This type of new dramaturgy instead of inciting an identification, aspires to the spectator's *disidentification*, "a strategy that tries to transform a cultural logic from within, always laboring to enact permanent structural change while at the same time valuing the importance of local or everyday struggles of resistance"[10]. And without any doubt, Rapi's theatre is an act of cultural resistance.

George Sampatakakis
University of Patras

[9] Dwight Conquergood, *Beyond the Text: Toward a Performative Cultural Politics*, in Sheron J. Dailey (ed.) *The Future of Performance Studies: Visions and Revisions* National Communication Association, Annandale, VA 1998, (pp. 25-36), p. 26

[10] José Muñoz, *Disidentifications: Queers of Color and the Performance of Politics*, University of Minnesota Press, Minneapolis 1999, pp. 11-12

Characters

ARIS	An archetypal figure of youthful beauty. He doubles as GUARD.
THE DOMINATRIX	Forties. Tall, thin and elegant in an exaggerated way. Heavily made up. Owner of a high-class brothel.
THE PRIEST	Male. Forties. Intense presence, yet also serene. Wears only a collar.
THE MERCENARY	Male. Forties. Powerful looking – has the nervous tics of a heavy smoker, gnaws his nails and shifts about when he talks.
THE ANOREXIC	Female. Twenty something; a strange mix of the saintly and the demonic.
THE BODYBUILDER	Female. Twenty something. Incongruously feminine.
THE BODYGUARD	Female. Early thirties. Very confident & attractive butch.
VOICE OVER	The voice of absolute authority – smoothly confident.
TIME	The timeless present.
BEAT	Indicates a brief pause and/or change of tone or mood.
/	Indicates interruption.
SETTING	A mindscape alluding to prison/ research lab or the reverse.
NOTE	Question of ARIS. It must be clear that ARIS is a memory, a presence felt by the PRIEST, DOMINATRIX & MERCENARY at different moments. That 'presence felt' is what should be enacted.

1

Snapshots of each character except for ARIS, front and profiles are projected on to a screen at the back of the stage, in rapid succession.

The MERCENARY is violently thrown onto the stage. He tries to maintain his macho posture. He regains his composure and looks around to establish where he is. He decides to sit and wait and looks as if he is sitting on hot bricks.

The DOMINATRIX enters next, slipping through an unseen grip. She paces up and down establishing control of the situation, setting her clothes and hair in order, regaining her confident poise. Looks around, notices the MERCENARY. They recognize each other and nod coldly. She sits coolly as far away from him as possible. Waits.

The PRIEST enters next, as if there by his own reluctant accord. He looks around apprehensively. Sees the DOMINATRIX, recognizes her and looks disturbed. She gives a Mona Lisa smile. He does not reciprocate. Instead, he coolly but politely greets both, then sits very much apart and waits, lost in painful thoughts.

The BODYBUILDER enters next, dressed in exaggerated feminine clothes, looking almost like a drag-queen. Her body language is very appeasing as she is getting her bearings. She is a little too cheerful as she greets the audience, clearly trying to hide extreme nervousness. She then parades front stage, poses and waits, looking the personification of a paradox – all muscles, yet little-girl mannerisms.

The BODYGUARD enters next, acting as if here for a formal enquiry of not much consequence to her but she can't quite conceal an inner terror. She checks things out. She recognizes the BODYBUILDER, smiles at her but the BODYBUILDER ignores her. The BODYGUARD shrugs and strikes an arrogant pose, waiting.

The ANOREXIC enters last, all edgy and paranoid. She scans everybody, recognizes and nods to the BODYGUARD who nods back. The ANOREXIC scrutinizes the BODYBUILDER and the PRIEST with curiosity, then wraps herself up in a foetus position.

Silence.

Beautiful blue light.

VOICE OVER Electro-magnetic fields imperceptibly invading
brain cells, nerve centers,
communication channels,
steadily breaking down defence mechanisms.
That's all.

A blast of futuristic rhythmic sounds, then abrupt stop.

VOICE OVER There is no smoke without fire. That's a fact.
Yet smoking guns are not what we are after.
What we are after is the truth –
truth extraction to be precise.
What we are after is guilt –
guilt erosion to be concise.
And we couldn't achieve this without you.
So thank you for being here.

Without you, we are nothing, in other words.
But let us not forget
that you are nothing without us.

Silence.

MERCENARY They're fucking with our heads, they are.

BODYGUARD Clever boy.

MERCENARY I beg your pardon?

BODYGUARD Fast thinking.

MERCENARY Listen you.

BODYBUILDER *(Shakes her ear up as a gesture of contempt.)*

MERCENARY Don't push it, right?

BODYGUARD You're scaring me.

*The MERCENARY makes to go for her. The BODYGUARD gets
ready, she loves a fight. The PRIEST stands between them.*

PRIEST   There's no need for this.

The MERCENARY retreats angrily.

The BODYGUARD grins triumphantly.

DOMINATRIX   *(Sucks her teeth.)* Such easy victims.

Silence.

MERCENARY   What the fuck do we do now?

PRIEST   Wait.

MERCENARY   Fuck me triple. How do you do *that*?

PRIEST   Watch me. *('Waits.')*

MERCENARY   *(Watches for a few seconds. Then moves about.)*
And what do they mean by all this?

PRIEST   That they know and control everything, I suppose.

DOMINATRIX   They know *less* than they seem to.
That's why we are here.

ANOREXIC   Nothing I say ever matters, anyway.

BODYBUILDER I'm only here by mistake.

BODYGUARD   Yeah, and my name is Brad Pitt.

*BODYBUILDER stares at her. BODYGUARD is pleased with
the reaction and stares back. BODYBUILDER looks away.
BODYGUARD puffs up.*

ANOREXIC feels she needs to defend the BODYBUILDER:

ANOREXIC   I'm one big, walking mistake, me.

*Bars descent in front of each character, trapping them in
inter-connected cells.*

The ANOREXIC looks terrified.

MERCENARY   What the fuck is this!

BODYGUARD   Jesus fucking Christ.

PRIEST   This is unnecessary.

DOMINATRIX   So unsophisticated. Really. *(Sucks her teeth.)*

The ANOREXIC's and the PRIEST's cells are next to each other. They look at each other. They form a silent bond. The PRIEST stretches his hand out and holds hers, reassuring her. She accepts this gratefully.

Extreme changes of light and temperature take place very rapidly. The characters are freezing one second, sweating the next; in total darkness one second, blinded by brilliant white light the next – all accompanied by a cacophony of sounds. By the end, they look disorientated, disturbed.

Beautiful melodies and a soft blue light suffuse the stage.

Enter the GUARD who ritualistically administers pills, then takes the CHARACTERS out of the cells, with a certain kind of kindness. The cells are withdrawn.

The CHARACTERS are gradually regaining some sort of composure.

What follows is in effect an echo of the beginning of the resolution. These are the voices within the characters' heads that have propelled them to this state. It's as if the truth is dying to get out of them through a repetition of these words. The CHARACTERS are however only aware of their voices as external voices, not belonging to them, at this point. While the CHARACTERS are speaking their lines, the external voices should be pre-recorded and heard as coming from a number of directions and on rising and falling volume levels, some could be repeated or echoed.

ANOREXIC   It's not guilt.
                 I learnt guilt before I even learned to speak.
                 Guilt is part of what I'm made of,
                 something I can handle.
                 So. It's not guilt. It's not fear either.
                 I learned fear the moment I learned to speak.

Fear feels like home. So. It's not fear either.
(Pause.)
It's doubt. That's what's killing me.

BODYGUARD She wanted to break the ice, she said,
the ice that kept me trapped,
the ice that kept me from feeling
all the love she could give me, all the.
Fuck. I can't deal with this shit.

BODYBUILDER I didn't punish him though,
not the way he used to punish me.
That would be taking advantage
of a sick, old man. I couldn't do that.

PRIEST Aris is calmly waiting for me to stop breathing....
It's like fighting a useless battle.
Yet something inside you,
survival instinct I suppose, urges you on.
Urges you on to fight. And you fight.
And I fought. I fought to start breathing again,
to come back to *this* reality.
And I did, I came back... *Without him...*

DOMINATRIX His games became more and more dangerous.
He pushed things, he pushed *me* to the edge.
That's where he felt most alive.
'This is real', he'd tell me,
'everything else is a delusion'.

MERCENARY I'd been in some deep shit in my life,
but I'd never felt scared. Not until then. *(Pause.)*
There was something about that boy's face
that freaked me out.
I've got to finish this job, I told myself,
I've got to finish it!

Blackout.

2

The stage is now divided in two levels. On the top level stand the PRIEST, the DOMINATRIX and the MERCENARY. On the lower level are the ANOREXIC, the BODYBUILDER and the BODYGUARD. The cells have gone. While action focuses on one trio, the other is silently watching the others, as if a chorus.

The MERCENARY is fidgeting, eating his nails. The DOMINATRIX is fixing her make up. The PRIEST is watching her.

PRIEST   Do you ever question what you do?

DOMINATRIX   What I do serves a useful purpose.

PRIEST   And what purpose would that be?

DOMINATRIX   I'm a healer, I treat sick minds.
With a philosophy degree under my belt,
I'm the ideal person to provide
the high class services that I do,
to the 'special' men that I get.
Coming to me desperate to find themselves,
to stand up to a world
that never asks them what they really want.

The PRIEST is deeply hurt by this exchange, perceiving it as a personal attack. DOMINATRIX is aware of this and means it this way.

DOMINATRIX   A world that holds them by the throat,
stretches them out on torture racks,
whips them into submission.
But they don't call holding you by the throat
a choking experience. And they don't call
the torture racks, torture racks.
And they don't call whipping you into submission,
whipping you into submission.

So. They get confused. My clients.
They feel choked but no one is choking them.
They feel pain but no one is whipping them,
you see?

PRIEST   And you…ease that 'pain'?

DOMINATRIX   I do more than that.
                  I help them to clear their heads,
                  to make those torture racks real,
                  to make that whip a real whip,
                  to make their external reality
                  match their internal reality.
                  That makes them feel sane and strong.

PRIEST   Aris…

DOMINATRIX   Yes?

PRIEST   He was too sensitive for you.

DOMINATRIX   He was much tougher than you thought.

PRIEST   You shouldn't have pushed him to such/

DOMINATRIX   And where did *you* push him to?

He stares at her. She stares back in defiance.

Cross fade to:

The BODYBUILDER is exercising obsessively. The ANOREXIC watches mesmerized. The BODYBUILDER welcomes this. Their dynamic excludes the BODYGUARD.

BODYGUARD   Stop staring at her for fuck's sake.

ANOREXIC   (*Her eyes keep darting from the BODYGUARD to the BODYBUILDER.*)
                  There was this girl opposite my flat.
                  Her body was perfect.
                  Pure muscle, not an ounce of flesh on her.
                  I loved watching her work that body.
                  She had a gym in her house, windows wide open,
                  summer and winter. Strange girl.

The BODYBUILDER exercises even more obsessively as she doesn't like what she's hearing.

ANOREXIC *(Examines BODYBUILDER curiously.)*
She had iron bars all over the place though,
doors, windows, everywhere.
I haven't seen her for a while.
I wonder what happened to her.

BODYGUARD Why don't you ask *me*.

ANOREXIC I don't want to. *(Beat.)*
Really, what I want, above all else, is to be myself,
the way I feel inside, Peter Pan,
the boy that can fly away from all this...
(Looks at her body with disgust. Beat.)
Mirror, mirror on the wall!

BODYGUARD 'ere. Look in my eyes if you want a fucking
mirror. What do you see?

ANOREXIC *(Looks for a moment.)* You looking at me.
(Turns to the BODYBUILDER.)
Don't you ever get tired?

BODYBUILDER You have to be very disciplined in my field.

ANOREXIC Discipline is my middle name.

BODYBUILDER *(Kindly ignores this.)*
But beauty is important too.
Bodybuilding is an opinion sport.
The more attractive you look,
the better chances you have of winning.

ANOREXIC Win. Win. Win. I always get what I want.
I can go for days without a milkshake.

BODYBUILDER Dad had me well trained from day one.

ANOREXIC I never knew my father.
Mother picked him up one day
and dropped him the next.

BODYGUARD Jesus.

BODYBUILDER I owe my success to dad.
I mean, *he* taught me to do
what *had* to be done...

BODYGUARD Sad fucker.

BODYBUILDER *(Looks at her askance and continues.)*
Dad had very strict rules about everything.
And I always obeyed them, no questions asked.
Because if I didn't, the lashes of his belt
would make sure I did.

ANOREXIC I never obey any rules. I'm free, me.
I can eat if I want to, I can starve if I want to,
I can binge if I want to, I can puke if I want to,
I can just. I can do what I like.

BODYBUILDER *(Looks at her in disguised condescension.)*
Well, I had to do what *he* liked.
Sometimes I couldn't obey his rules
through no fault of my own but
because he had changed them in the meantime.
He'd only do that to keep me on my toes.
So if I hadn't caught on,
I deserved punishment.
He was a good teacher dad, really.
Taught me to watch myself.

ANOREXIC choc chunks, double choc chunk cookies,
triple choc chunk cookies,
choc choc chunk chunk cookies cookies,
choc choc

BODYGUARD You're a fucking pair of nuts you two.

BODYBUILDER Will you stop following me around?

BODYGUARD I never follow anyone unless I'm paid for it,
sweetheart. And daddy can't exactly write
a cheque these days, can he now?

The BODYBUILDER stares at her angrily, then pointedly ignores her and turns to the ANOREXIC, who's not stopped watching her.

BODYBUILDER *(To the ANOREXIC.)* And you.
Will you stop staring?

ANOREXIC I wasn't, I was just wondering/

BODYBUILDER /Just leave me alone, ok?

The ANOREXIC looks hurt and withdraws.

The BODYGUARD grins.

Slow fade.

3

The ANOREXIC, hurt, has shifted her attention to the BODYGUARD.

The BODYBUILDER exercises her body in various poses but listens too.

ANOREXIC I wish I were luckier with girls.

BODYGUARD Take a leaf from my book, babes.

ANOREXIC Yeah? Like how?

BODYGUARD *(Performing.)*
You've got to learn how to satisfy a woman.
It's an art.
No girl has ever been through my hands,
other than fully satisfied.
And I don't just mean
'that was really nice, thank you.'
I mean: 'I've never been had this way before.
Don't ever leave me, Josie,' and the like.
But of course I always do.
It's not that I like breaking their hearts or anything.
I'm always on the level with them.
Don't get hooked on me girl,
you'll only hurt yourself, I always say.
But do they listen? Do they fuck.

BODYBUILDER comes closer, pays attention.

ANOREXIC looks pleased.

BODYGUARD I believe in being honest.

BODYBUILDER 'Sir' always believes in fantasies.

ANOREXIC Sir?

BODYGUARD Yeah, 'sir'. Let her babble.
You know what I like best?
Riding my Harley like a bullet
then parking it really slow
outside any bar I fancy and
make like I don't see all those hungry eyes,
eating me alive,
eyes that can't tell whether I'm a man or a woman.
I get a kick out of that.

BODYBUILDER You would.

BODYGUARD I had a contract with *that* cop's daughter once.
(Points at the BODYBUILDER.)

BODYBUILDER makes to say something, changes her mind.

ANOREXIC *(Watches with increased interest.)*
Your dad is a cop?

BODYGUARD Why don't you ask me? That's what I'm here for.

BODYBUILDER You're here for your own shit.

BODYGUARD I've got no shit, darling.
I'm clean like spring water, me.

BODYBUILDER grins and turns to the ANOREXIC.

BODYBUILDER So what if my dad is a *Police Commissioner.*

ANOREXIC makes a conciliatory gesture.

BODYGUARD *(Looks at the BODYBUILDER provocatively.)*

81

She was weird. She couldn't tell her pussies
from her willies that girl.
Now, I may look like I could be either
but, really, a close look
will leave you with no doubt I'm female.
She couldn't see that.
She kept calling me 'sir'. Daddy's girl. Stupid.

*BODYBUILDER looks back angrily, is about to say something,
decides against it again.*

ANOREXIC keeps staring at the BODYBUILDER.

BODYGUARD   Stop staring at her and listen to me.

ANOREXIC   Listening.

BODYGUARD   The biggest fun is in women's toilets.
I always have a good laugh there.
'There's a man in the toilet', they scream
and in comes security.
'Where is he?' I says. 'I'm having none of this
young man, out you go.'
'Don't insult me,' I says, and I flash them my tits.
Ah, ouch, giggle, giggle. 'Sorry sir, ah, madam.'
'That's alright, darling,' I goes,
and play it all offended.
I then burst out laughing.
Why are people so screwed up
about this man, woman thing, I ask you.

BODYBUILDER finds the question ridiculous.

ANOREXIC   I'm not. I'm a boy too! Peter Pan!

BODYGUARD   'Course you are babes.

ANOREXIC   Peter Pan – flyiiiing awaaaaaay.

BODYGUARD   Yeah, sure. Anyhow – it's useful
looking the way I do, neither man nor woman.
It's very handy when you're a bodyguard.

You've got to look like you mean business,
like you take no shit,
like you can break a bone or two. *(Looking at
the BODYBUILDER's heels.)* And you can't do this
on high heels, can you now?

BODYBUILDER dismisses this as juvenile bragging.

BODYGUARD *(To the ANOREXIC.)*
So what I'm saying to you, babes, is this:
women like you to be tough and ambiguous.

ANOREXIC Do they? *(Beat.)* How come you never told me
you knew *her*?

BODYGUARD Wasn't meant to, babes. Daddy's orders.

ANOREXIC I thought you were my friend.

BODYGUARD In a manner of speaking... In that I like you.
But I was doing a job. It's what I do.
Watch over people. Usually they know.
But with you it was meant to be a bloody secret.
He didn't want you two to know/

BODYBUILDER Shut up!

ANOREXIC choc chunks, double choc chunk cookies,
triple choc chunk cookies,
choc choc, chunk chunk, cookies cookies,
choc choc

Cross fade to:

PRIEST *(To the MERCENARY.)* Did you not think
you were taking a huge risk with the boy?

MERCENARY Don't get personal, mate. Not a good idea,
take my word for it.

PRIEST considers this.

DOMINATRIX Risk-taking is essential in *my* work.

PRIEST Doesn't safety come into this? Responsibility?

DOMINATRIX: I am a firm believer in safety measures
and taking responsibility for your actions.

PRIEST Well then?

DOMINATRIX Well, then we're talking about pleasure.
When it comes to pleasure, darling,
responsibility lies with the pleasure seeker
not the pleasure provider,
especially with a professional of my standing.
The pleasure seeker must be aware of
and state his limits. *(Beat.)*
It's my duty, of course, to safeguard those limits.
And I always do.

PRIEST *(Icily.)* Then why didn't you,
when it mattered the most?

DOMINATRIX I can't be held responsible for my clients' actions.
(Beat.) If pleasure is more important to them
than safety, who am I to disagree?

PRIEST Don't you feel any remorse?

DOMINATRIX I'm a pro.

MERCENARY So am I. We are a different breed, us. *(Beat.)*
But some of them pros are fucking animals,
I tell you,
ripping off ears from dead bodies
to sell to the UN soldiers for souvenirs.
Diabolical.
Me, I never violate a dead body.
There's a line I won't cross.

PRIEST Is *this* where you cross the line?

MERCENARY Mate, you'd better not/

*DOMINATRIX is interrupting him as if answering on his behalf/
defending him and resuming her attack on the PRIEST at the
same time.*

DOMINATRIX   The only lines *I* draw
are to do with maximizing pleasure.
I do like to give them my all.
I've got a reputation to keep but beyond that
it simply gives me pleasure to give pleasure.
(Beat.)
And I do have a weakness for boys, I must say.

PRIEST   Was that all it was then? A 'weakness' for boys?

DOMINATRIX   Don't you like boys yourself?

PRIEST   I liked Aris. That's different.
(Beat. To the MERCENARY.)
And you? What was it for you?

MERCENARY   You're asking the wrong question, mate.
Listen to what I'm gonna say in case you get
the picture. I was at work, right?
Minding my own business.
Some prisoners had been taken, just farmers really
and one of them was thought to be a spy, right?
They took him into a room, with a colonel,
and they were slapping him,
burning him with cigarettes,
beating him with coshes,
sticking a knife in his cheek.
Then they took him outside
and chopped his fucking head off
and brought it in to show the colonel.

I just sat and watched. What can you do?
I'd come in with a briefing.
I mean, you're thinking
that's how the cookie crumbles,
it's a two way street,
there's two sides to every story, isn't?
I'm a pro. I'm just doing my job.

PRIEST   Is this how you comfort yourself?

MERCENARY   Don't like your tone there, mate.

DOMINATRIX *(Continuing as before.)* It's all part of the game.
Putting them on racks, in isolation, in chains,
whipping them, gagging them, torturing them.
(Beat.)
They love it of course *(Beat.)*
It's my duty to oblige.
I do it with the same precision
a surgeon does a heart transplant.
We're talking major operation here.
Lives are at stake.
A mistake, you understand, may be fatal.
So I don't make mistakes. *(Beat.)*
And I don't like to be blamed.

PRIEST I'm not blaming you.

DOMINATRIX You are.

PRIEST I just want to understand...

DOMINATRIX looks at him as if for the first time. She seems to feel empathy.

DOMINATRIX It will take time...

Silence.

MERCENARY You've got to listen, mate,
if you want to understand us.
You wanna hear more?

PRIEST nods yes.

MERCERARY Right. Listen to this.
I trained some dodgy outfits, I tell you,
long-hairs, rock and rollers, you name it.
Got a nice buzz from turning a bunch of no-goods
into 'units' that could really handle a Kalashnikov.
Turned them into real soldiers.
I taught them no-goods professionalism, discipline.
Discipline is crucial, mate,
if you want things to run smoothly.
And you want that, believe me,

if you want pros fighting next to you.
(Beat.) What about you?
When did you decide to… *(Imitates prayer.)*

PRIEST   You really want to know?

MERCENARY Got to keep talking, mate.
That's the name of the game here.
Got to keep talking. Keep talking!

DOMINATRIX Go on, tell us!

PRIEST   *(Considers. Decides.)* I was a 'man of the world',
I lived without any sense of mean and measure…

MERCENARY No kidding.

PRIEST   Going from dark and dirty corner
to dark and dirty corner
craving sex like a vampire craves blood,
not a word spoken, not a tender whisper.

MERCENARY You don't need that shit anyhow, do you?

PRIEST   I do, I need that 'shit'. It got to the point when
I couldn't even remember how many men I've
had or who I went with. It felt so futile.
Took away the thrill of sex.

DOMINATRIX Nothing can take away the thrill of sex.

PRIEST   For you maybe…it made *me* feel reduced
to a cluster of nerve endings.
Not quite a state of grace. I felt that a
cockroach had more purpose than me.

DOMINATRIX So… Is this when you changed?

PRIEST   That's right. Get ordained, man, and abstain,
that's the answer, I told myself.
Free yourself. No more bondage
to constant craving… *(Smiles.)*
No more dependence
on the sexual hunger of strangers.

DOMINATRIX I always depend on the sexual hunger of strangers...

MERCENARY And then what?

PRIEST Meditation, prayer and the company of like-minded people gave me strength and a new sense of purpose.
I was no longer the slave of my body but its master. *(Beat.)*
I *am* no longer the slave of my body but its master.

DOMINATRIX A mistake, that was a mistake you know that now, don't you?

PRIEST It was not a mistake.

DOMINATRIX You can't turn your back on pleasure.
Pleasure is the last freedom in these days of boxed in, shackled up, all dead inside nobodies who pass for good citizens...
And I get lots of them, believe me. *(Beat.)*
Along with the special ones...like Aris...

PRIEST If he were special,
why didn't you treat him as such?

DOMINATRIX A more special treatment, I can't imagine.
I gave him the ultimate gift.

PRIEST How can you call it that?

DOMINATRIX *shrugs defiantly. The* PRIEST *feels caged.*

MERCENARY *is looking at the* PRIEST, *trying to figure him out.*

He has touched him somewhere but he can't quite figure it out.

Slow fade.

4

BODYBUILDER works her muscles, ignoring the other two.

ANOREXIC   I don't think she likes you.

BODYGUARD   Most women like me, babes,
even if they don't show it or know it…
'cos I know how to please them, you get me?

BODYBUILDER joins them, unaware of what has been said.

BODYGUARD winks at ANOREXIC.

BODYGUARD   Now, that's bound to make some crypto dykes
jealous.

BODYBUILDER   If you mean me, you're way off target.

BODYGUARD   Didn't say you, sweetheart.
I was just telling a story.
So, as I was saying. I've noticed
how some people get all sour
when they see you scoring the best trade.
Sometimes they get more than sour.
They interfere.
Like that night at the Pussy Club.
(Takes up more space for a 'performance'.)

ANOREXIC   I've been there.

BODYGUARD   I know you've been there, babes.
I took you there myself.
Now, listen to this.

ANOREXIC   Listening.

BODYGUARD   There was I dancing with that night's score
when this shaved-head number
starts eyeing my girl.
I give her a filthy look, she takes no notice.
I swirl my girl around and
give baldie a push on the way,
she gets the message.

Later, I go to get a drink at the bar
and when I turn around what do I see?
Baldie's cruising my girl well and truly,
right under my nose.
Now, that's more than disrespectful in my book.
It's sheer provocation. I just see red.
And I head-butt her without thinking.
My girl is speechless. But proud of me, I can see.
What the fuck. You've got to protect your catch.

Long pause. Stops performing. Seems to be sinking into thought.

ANOREXIC   Protect your 'catch'. How can you talk like this about your lover?

BODYGUARD   That girl was really special, I must say.

The BODYBUILDER looks with interest.

ANOREXIC   And where is that girl now?

BODYGUARD   What?

ANOREXIC   Where is *she* now?

BODYGUARD   How the fuck should I know. *(Walks away.)*

ANOREXIC   Where are you going? Come back!

BODYGUARD   *(Comes back.)* Tell me babes.

ANOREXIC   What?

BODYGUARD   Do you think I've done something wrong?

ANOREXIC   How would I know?

BODYGUARD   You know about these things. You're brainy.

ANOREXIC   What kind of wrong, to whom and by whom? You've got to be specific.

BODYGUARD   Don't get all nerdy on me, now.

Just answer me straight.

ANOREXIC Well, with the little you're giving me,
all I can tell you is what's the *worst* kind of
wrong.

BODYGUARD What's that then?

ANOREXIC It's the kind of wrong you can't forgive yourself for.

BODYGUARD Fucking great. Ask a weirdo a question,
you get a weird answer.

BODYBUILDER That got you, didn't it?

*BODYGUARD withdraws into a corner. Her inner terror begins
to surface. She battles with her rising thoughts and feelings,
trying to stay in control. The BODYBUILDER feels stronger by
this, approaches the ANOREXIC who is only too glad.*

BODYBUILDER You really got her there… See this?
(Shows a scar on her left thigh.) I did this myself.
(Beat.) Just to prove that I can do it
without flinching.

ANOREXIC Well, me, I've got a hole in my belly, me,
it's really BIG. *(Beat.)*
Nothing can fill it. Ever. The only thing that can
fill this hole is mmmmmmoth, MOTHER!
Oops, there I said it.

BODYBUILDER I never knew my mother.

BODYGUARD comes back.

BODYBUILDER 'Sir' is back. My bodyguard. Ha.
Left her and dad and became a free woman.

BODYGUARD Got another job straight away. From your dad.

BODYBUILDER That's a lie.

BODYGUARD That's a fact.

BODYBUILDER It's a lie! *(Beat.)* Dad didn't take well to me not
talking to him. *(Beat.)*
But sometimes, it's best to just keep away.

ANOREXIC   I could never leave home. How could I?
It'd have killed mum.

BODYBUILDER You keep away out of love, not to hurt.

ANOREXIC   I couldn't hurt a fly.
I couldn't even kill a cockroach
and they repulse me.

BODYGUARD Such pure white lilies you both are.
You know, it was you *her* dad,
your dad, asked me to watch over.

ANOREXIC   chunks, double choc chunk cookies, triple choc
chunk cookies, choc
choc, chunk chunk, cookies cookies, choc choc

BODYGUARD Will you two fucking listen!

BODYBUILDER Nothing to hear.

ANOREXIC   chunk chunk cookies cookies, choc choc
chunk chunk

BODYGUARD Stop this psycho stuff.

ANOREXIC   chunk chunk cookies cookies, choc choc
chunk chunk

BODYGUARD Fuck's sake. *(Beat.)* Your father...
her father, one and the same.
He paid me to look after you
when she disappeared.
He couldn't take it, having no one to watch over...
The sad fucker.

The BODYBUILDER *looks at her angrily.*

ANOREXIC   I never knew my father.
Mother picked him up one night
and dropped him the next.

BODYGUARD Your mother was with him for years.
He left her when you were a baby, left with her.

(Shows the BODYBUILDER.) She was just a little
older than you.
They split you up.
But he kept providing.
Where do you think all the money came from?
Your mother never worked.
Nor you for that matter.

ANOREXIC chunk chunk cookies cookies, choc choc
chunk chunk

BODYBUILDER You're full of shit. It's all lies.

BODYGUARD Oh yeah?

BODYBUILDER What happened to that girl then?

BODYGUARD It's none of your business.

ANOREXIC chunk chunk cookies cookies, choc choc
chunk chunk

BODYBUILDER What happened to that girl?
Why don't you tell us?
What happened?

The BODYGUARD pretends not to hear but seems deeply
affected. Moves away.

Slow fade.

5

The PRIEST, DOMINATRIX and the MERCENARY are seated in silence. The PRIEST wants an answer; the DOMINATRIX is defiant; the MERCENARY is wondering how the hell he is going to get out of all this.

ANOREXIC is curled up in a foetus position, staring ahead. BODYBUILDER is embracing her body, shivering. BODYGUARD is leaning against a wall, trying hard not to show her rising inner terror.

VOICE OVER Sodium pentothal enhancing the brain's sensitivity
to the depressant neurotransmitter Gaba,
steadily instilling fear, disorientation,
gradually revealing what's hidden…
and finally forcing the truth out!

Enter the GUARD playing the flute. He circles the CHARACTERS. He stops playing music, administers tablets.

VOICE OVER Fear not, ladies and gentlemen,
for this is pure soul medicine.

The CHARACTERS are swallowing tablets manically. Their bodies gradually reshape from disorientation & fear into some sort of acceptance of their situation/resignation, into a confessional mode.

Question of ARIS here. It must be clear that ARIS is a memory, a presence felt by the PRIEST, DOMINATRIX & MERCENARY at different moments. That 'presence felt' is what should be enacted.

During each following monologue, the faces of the characters are projected on a back screen, capturing minutiae of their expressions. Unless otherwise stated, the characters are addressing the audience, under a single spotlight each, unless there is dialogue.

MERCENARY It was an interesting job, the money was good,
five grand for blowing up a factory,
ten for poisoning water tanks,
and twenty for training the private armies of
drug cartels.
I liked the risk, the action, getting down to it,
not sitting in some poncy office,
watching things on a screen,
giving orders over the telephone.
You handle real stuff like rocket launchers,
fragmentation grenades, stripped-down cars
with anti-aircraft guns welded to the boot,
not a fucking keyboard.
I had the balls to go out there
and do the thing, gunpowder in your nostrils,
no fucking joke.

Helped, me serving in the Paras and all that.
Had a tough regiment though, I tell you.
No prisoners.
Kill 'em and let God sort 'em out.
You're in a fucking battlefield,
what do you expect?
The rules are quite simple:
if you start taking liberties,
you'll be fucking court martialled in the field,
tried by three professional soldiers
and if you're found guilty you'll be executed.
You're in the front line for fuck's sake,
you learn to obey the rules or else.

PRIEST There can be no closer
to how close me and Aris were...
But he wanted more of me than I could give...

It wasn't his age.
He was above the age of consent.
It wasn't even the fact that
I had taken my celibacy vows.

He was worth breaking those vows for. *(Pause.)*
It was something else entirely...

MERCENARY Got a medical discharge. Bastards.
Nothing wrong with me.
Lucky another war soon broke out.
Always does, somewhere. Always does.
Civil war that one.
They came to me from both sides.
Could have gone with both but
wouldn't risk it from the security point of view.
Got another medical discharge,
what's the fucking matter with them?
Anyhow, in the end they made me an offer
somewhere else, an offer I had to refuse.
I'm no fucking cripple, I said.
There are lines I won't cross, mate.

DOMINATRIX He started visiting me at a point in my life
when I needed to feel young.
I'd never felt young. I was born old.
And I liked that. Until I turned forty.
I wanted to feel young all of a sudden.
And feel youthful energy around me.
(Pause.) His energy.

PRIEST He loved talking about his dreams.
They were more real to him than real life.
'You are the closest to what I feel in my dreams,'
he told me once. 'You too,'
I nearly said but felt I shouldn't.
And I didn't. I could feel his disappointment
at my lack of response...
It lingered in the blackness of his eyes,
then sinking inside him, turning into
God knows what demon, what fury...
I wished at that moment
he'd just lash out
at me instead...
filled me up with blood...

bruises and broken bones...
anything but *that disappointed look...*

DOMINATRIX   He went from client to lover in no time.
He was gentle, so gentle in fact
it was almost disturbing.
He was the only one who could
outwit me in my games.
And it was pure instinct on his part.
That *look* on his face!
Apologetic and defiant at the same time for
having got there first. That was his game.
Out-maneuver and be punished for winning.
How could I resist?

PRIEST   I hadn't seen my sister for many years.
I had no time for family then...
She'd broken up with her husband,
a right brute, whom I had never met.
He'd lash out at them until he was unconscious
with frenzy.
She left him. That's when I last saw them.
And now, years later, they came to find me.
Her and Aris.
My sister's son.
My deliverance.
The forbidden fruit.

The last time I'd seen him he was a child.
Now he was a man. A boyish man. A mannish boy.
With fire in his belly and a riddle in his eyes.

When my sister went off travelling,
she wanted to see the world she said,
Aris asked me if he could stay with me.
I couldn't refuse him that.
I hadn't realized at the time how much
he wanted to be with me.
I thought he simply wanted to explore the new city.

DOMINATRIX   His games became more and more dangerous.
He pushed things, he pushed *me* to the edge.
That's where he felt most alive.
'This is real, everything else is a delusion,'
he'd tell me.

PRIEST   There was relief. Oh yes.
There was sweet delusion.
Who was it that said?
'Delusions hold us together,
reality will tear us apart.' Apt so apt.
I was under the delusion he had accepted
that our love could only be spiritual.
And he was under the delusion that he
would persuade me in time
to love him the way he wanted to.

So. We stayed together for a year,
our delusions holding us together. *(Beat.)*
The madness in his eyes when he realized
I'd never, *ever* agree to sexual love.

His eyes said more than words could ever say,
eyes that stripped you bare
grabbed you by the throat
held you hostage
begging for mercy.

MERCENARY   There was something about that boy's eyes
I'd not seen before.
Anywhere. On anyone. Except perhaps. *(Beat.)*
He looked at me in a way
that made me feel all shaky,
kind of scared. Now, that's well unlike me.
I'd been in some deep shit in my life
but I'd never felt scared. Not until then.

DOMINATRIX   He had a way of bringing alive
parts of my self that were long dead and buried,
making me feel more real
than I had for a long time.

I don't know how it happened.
And it happened quickly.
He just sort of slipped into my blood-stream
you could say.
It got to the point that
if I wanted a good look at myself,
all I had to do was look at him.

MERCENARY There comes a point when you do some jobs
where something tells you,
you shouldn't be doing this.
But you're a professional. So, you do it.
You do it, no matter what.

PRIEST No words
there are no words to describe
how you feel
when you see without eyes
talk without tongues
touch without skin.
(Pause. To the DOMINATRIX.) Did you love him?

DOMINATRIX Did I love him? What is love anyway?
Wanting to give pleasure more
than wanting to receive it,
that's love I suppose. So, in that sense, yes.
But it was more than that...
(Beat.) He...*was* definitely unique.
I wouldn't want to lose him...
and that's the closest I've ever been to love –
in the conventional sense... Yes, I loved him.
But it was more than love he made me feel.
He broke the rules. Reversed the roles.
He topped me by daring me
to do things I'd never done before.
No one else had risked that before,
eager to submit, they just complied
to my demands.

It gets tiring...after a while. He saw that.
And pushed me to the edge.
It felt like...freedom. *(Long pause.)*
And you? Did *you* love him?

PRIEST   The Sufis believe they commune with God
by looking into the eyes of the Beloved...
I know it sounds O.T.T. but it was like that
between me and Aris...
(To the DOMINATRIX.) You took that away.

DOMINATRIX   I only take what belongs to me.

PRIEST   He didn't belong to you.

DOMINATRIX   If the person you loved the most,
the only person who ever made you feel free,
asked you to release him from a shackle
only you could release him from,
would you refuse?

PRIEST   You had no right...

DOMINATRIX   *You* drove him to *me*... I'm grateful for that...

The PRIEST is hurt profoundly by this. Silence.

DOMINATRIX   We were made of the same kind of stuff. Inside.

PRIEST   That's what I believed too...

DOMINATRIX   You held back, I didn't...

PRIEST   I had to.

DOMINATRIX   You never *have to* do anything.
There is always choice. *(Beat.)*

You don't meet people like that everyday.
And when you do,
you bond in ways that other people
can't understand.
You bond in ways that make you do things
other people can't understand.

You bond in ways that make you do things
you'd never otherwise do.

PRIEST   You shouldn't have. You simply shouldn't.

DOMINATRIX I did.

Silence. They look at each other in defiant, controlled confrontation.

PRIEST   *(To the MERCENARY.)* And you?
Did you…bond with him…in any way?

MERCENARY You do sort of blood bond with the boys
in the field like.
But you don't want to bond too much,
it'd interfere with business, you'd be mad to…

Cross fade to:

BODYBUILDER When I was a kid, dad would just stand there,
upright as a pole,
watching me having a cold shower
in the middle of winter,
making sure I didn't turn the hot water on.
(Pause.)
Later, he'd stand by the door well into the night
watching me,
making sure I fell asleep without ever…
you know, touching myself.
He did this until I left home for college. *(Beat.)*
Dad loved me, there's no doubt about that.
Everything he did, he did it out of love for me.
Protection.

ANOREXIC   Mirror, mirror on the wall,
who's the Thinnest of them all?
That's the first rhyme mother ever taught me.
She'd stand me in front of the mirror
before I even learned to walk,
and sing it with me, again and again…
(Standing in front of an imaginary mirror, singing.)

'Mirror, mirror on the wall,
who's the Thinnest of them all?'
'Mummy! Mummy's the Thinnest,'
was the right answer.
I've smashed quite a few mirrors in my life.
Tiny, pocket mirrors, wall-hanged mirrors,
full-body swing mirrors...
All liars!

I learned to speak in sentences, me.
So, no ma-ma-ma, ga-ga-ga for me.
Full sentences only. Like:
'Why's mummy crying again?'
'Because mummy doesn't want to be here,' was
the right answer. *(Beat.)*
I'd get a slap every time I got the answer wrong.
And I kept getting it wrong because it didn't
sound right.

BODYGUARD She wanted to break the ice, she said,
the ice that kept me trapped,
the ice that kept me from feeling
all the love she could give me, all the.
Fuck. I can't deal with this shit.

BODYBUILDER Daddy had me well trained from day one.

ANOREXIC I never knew my father.
Mother picked him up one night
and dropped him the next.

BODYGUARD Dream on.

ANOREXIC Mother wanted to abort me but
they insisted at the hospital that pregnancy
would cure her anorexia.
She didn't believe them. *(Beat.)*
But kept me anyway.
She must have cared...a little...

BODYBUILDER You don't appreciate this kind of discipline
when you're little.

But later you do. So, I said to myself:
Your dad loves you girl.
He's doing all this for a purpose.
He's training you for life.
Don't let all this discipline go to waste. Use it.
Use it to get out of here. So. That's what I did.

That's when I decided to stop talking to dad.
(Pause.) That's when I decided
to become a bodybuilder.
I felt free at the gym.
No more dad telling me what to do.
I was my own woman at last. *(Beat.)*

Only thing was I had to imagine him being there,
urging me on to try harder and harder.
Urging me the way only *he* knew how.
Lashing, lashing, lashing out at me.
But loving me all the while. Taking care of me.
It was the only way. And it worked.
That's how I became a champion.

(Beat. Defiantly.) If it helps me get ahead
imagining daddy
belting me to perfection,
well, what's wrong with that?

ANOREXIC   chunk chunk cookies cookies, choc choc
chunk chunk

Blackout.

6

A moment of silence. The CHARACTERS look as if waiting for permission to talk. The GUARD enters again playing the flute. He circles them, stops playing, lifts their heads as if they are puppets, administers tablets. The CHARACTERS respond as if they are puppets. Gradually they come alive.

BODYBUILDER Dad decided to get ill at the height of my career.
No, this sounds all wrong.
Dad got ill at a difficult time for me.
No, this isn't right either. (*Beat.*)
Dad was dying and I found it out by accident.
(*Beat.*)
I felt it was my fault he was ill.
I put the past behind me and ran to his side.
Once I got there, he didn't want to die anymore.
He had his daughter back, so he held on... (*Beat.*)
I couldn't train of course. I lost competitions,
my muscles got all loose and ugly,
my career went downhill.

BODYGUARD She was special that girl, no doubt about it.
Knew how to treat me, make me feel good...
So, I made the mistake of letting her get close.
Fucking scary. I started losing myself.
I had to fix it.
So, I said: that's it babes. It's over.
Can't go further than this.
Can you understand? No, she couldn't. (*Pause.*)
So. I stayed. It was a mega mistake to the
power of ten.
There were moments,
there were moments I admit,
when I thought I could get to like this.
But I felt kind of sick, you know?
Like when you're on the top of a building
and you look down and you get sick in the
stomach, you get all nauseous,
you lose your head. I had to stop it.
Now, she was a sensitive girl, I must say that.
She had kind of got attached to me.
Rooted more like it.
It was hard.
She wouldn't give up.

She wanted to break the ice, she said,
the ice that kept me trapped,
the ice that kept me from feeling
all the love she could give me, all the.
Fuck. I can't deal with this shit.

ANOREXIC It's not guilt.
I learnt guilt before I even learned to speak.
Guilt is part of what I'm made of,
something I can handle.
So. It's not guilt. It's not fear either.
I learned fear the moment I learned to speak.
Fear feels like home.
So. It's not fear either. *(Pause.)*
It's doubt. That's what's killing me.

BODYBUILDER Perhaps I shouldn't have
dropped out of college...
or chosen a career he hated...
and really I didn't need to stop talking to him...

ANOREXIC I just stopped eating and then
she stopped crying.
That was scary. Mother not crying.
It almost made me want to start eating again.
But I didn't. I couldn't. So, she stopped talking.

BODYBUILDER You don't get cancer because
your daughter has developed muscles, do you?
Of course not. *(Beat.)* Or because
she won't talk to you anymore.
Cancer is cancer is cancer.
It's a body thing.
If your body gives up on you,
there is nothing you can do about it.
All the daughters in the world
can't save you then.

ANOREXIC It's doubt. That's what's killing me.

BODYBUILDER Dad became more and more dependent on me.
I had to feed him, bathe him, change him.
It got to the point where he couldn't do a thing
by himself.

ANOREXIC If only I hadn't stopped eating.
That's when things started getting really bad.
(Beat.)
Or were they always bad?

BODYGUARD It wasn't easy. It's not easy to be hard
to someone so bloody soft and sensitive!

ANOREXIC She stopped crying and she stopped talking.
(Pause.)
The only thing mother ever talked about was
food…and calories…and body weight…
and how empty she felt inside.

BODYBUILDER He kept dropping and knocking things,
spilling drink and food all over the place,
getting his words mixed up…
I didn't punish him though,
not the way *he* used to punish me.
That would be taking advantage of a sick,
old man. I couldn't do that.

ANOREXIC I couldn't hurt her. I could never…
ops two 'I's together.
I… I…don't exist.

BODYGUARD I wanted to help her get over me.
But she didn't want to get over me.
She wanted me back. Plain and simple.
And I wasn't having it.
Love ain't my territory. *(Pause.)*

One night, it was three in the morning,
I'm off work, resting, and the phone rings.
It's her of course. She's in a state.
Let's talk things through, she says.

Nothing to talk about, babes, it's over.
Well and truly, over.
But I can't forget you, Josie.
I can't help you there, babes, you'll get used to it.
You loved me once, she says.
Maybe I did. But it never lasts with me
this kind of thing.

Did she hang up after this? Did she, fuck.
On and on about how much she loved me,
couldn't live without me, all that kind of stuff.

Now, I was used to this kind of talk
and I always handled it well in the past.
This time though, I blew my top.
'Listen, babes,' I shout, 'We've had what we had,
it's finished, you understand?
Finito. Caput. The end.'
And I slam the phone down.

She rings back, I put the answerphone on.
She begs me to answer that phone,
I wasn't having it.
She begs and cries and begs and cries,
I wasn't having it.
Suddenly she stops crying and hangs up.
I'm surprised. But I do nothing.

Silence.

ANOREXIC I wasn't eating because I wanted to live.
Mother stopped eating because
she wanted to die.
She took to her bed,
laid herself out as if in a coffin,
hands carefully folded over her chest and waited.

I tried talking her out of it but
she had made her mind up.
I could have called a doctor but it seemed wrong.
Mother looked content

for the first time in her life.
I decided to just sit by her and wait.

BODYGUARD The next day, something tells me
I should go around her flat.
(Long pause.)
The mess of it...blood all over the place.
CUT HER FUCKING WRISTS. *(Long pause.)*
I mean, Jesus, it wasn't my fault.
The girl was imbalanced.
(Long pause.) I mean, Jesus,
what did she go and do that for?
To teach me a lesson? *(Long pause.)*
Bloody hell, I admit, I can't deal with this
getting close shit.
(Pause.) Scary, fucking scary.
Makes no fucking sense. Ok. I plead guilty to that!
But what can I do?
Choke myself so as not to hurt her?

ANOREXIC She never looked at me once during those days.
One night though, she turned to me and smiled.
I knew the time had come. I smiled back.
I bent over and kissed her on the forehead.
She went like an angel.

BODYBUILDER In the end, he couldn't even talk.
Only his eyes stayed alive, telling me things
he'd never said before. Just by looking.
We never felt as close as we did then.
So he held on...and on...and on...and on...

It was difficult. I didn't want him to go...
but something inside me...
...one night, I decided...he wanted to go...
but I wasn't sure.
I asked him to make it clear.
I told him: eyes up means no,
eyes down, means yes.
He just looked at me, eyes neither up nor down

but looking straight at me.
He was leaving it up to me… I thought…
I increased his dose of morphine
explaining to him clearly
what I was doing…
what *had to be done…*

Slow fade.

7

The CHARACTERS are compulsively swallowing tablets as if their life depends on it, tablets administered by the GUARD with music, circling as before only more intense this time. The GUARD exits.

VOICE OVER   High dosages of propranolol released
into a dense knot of neurons,
the amygdala, tracing the shadows
of fear and memory,
penetrating the neural pathways
guilt and regret travel through,
thus obliterating them both.

When *guilt erosion* is fully accomplished,
you shall be free, my friends. Free!

Silence.

BODYBUILDER Father is dead, well and truly buried.
But not a moment goes by
that I don't see his eyes
begging me, begging me not to…not to…
NOT TO!
I should have never done that!
I must be punished. I must!

VOICE OVER   However, whenever there is resistance,
regrets persist and guilt refuses to be erased,
higher dosages become necessary,
running the risk of fatal consequences…

BODYBUILDER *(Defeated, deadpan.)* Punish me please,
I can't stand this!

VOICE OVER May I repeat: guilt must be absolutely eliminated!
However, a higher dose may prove fatal…

BODYBUILDER *(Same tone.)* Do whatever is necessary,
I can't take this!

Silence.

BODYGUARD I mean, if I knew she'd do that,
I'd have made an effort, wouldn't I?
I might have swallowed my fear,
this choking feeling. *(Beat.)*
But how do you do that?

Cross fade to:

MERCENARY I'd been out of work for a while.
As if you can't fucking handle a grenade when
you hit forty. Shit. Anyhow. No work.
And I don't like being out of action.
A 'walk up' contract would come in handy
right now, I thought,
but would have to be some really nasty fucker
or a serious paedophile or something.
Couldn't waste just anybody, not really. *(Beat.)*
I'd never had expected an offer like that
though, I must say.

*ARIS' words in the following section could be spoken by him
or spoken by him and the character speaking them, at the
same time – to be decided in rehearsal. Also, some of what
follows could be enacted by ARIS. Again, it's important that
this is acted out as 'memory'.*

DOMINATRIX 'It has to be an older man,' he said,
'in his forties. That's crucial.'

MERCENARY 'I need to think about it,' I said.
'Sounds too pervy for my taste.'

PRIEST   He packed his things, came to my room,
               looked at me for what seemed like forever
               and left without a word.
               Without anger, without joy, without pain.
               Just icy determination.
               He left without as much as a goodbye.

DOMINATRIX 'In his forties and capable of cold murder,
               without hesitation,' he said.
               'Capable of carrying out orders to the last detail.
               Can you find him for me?'

MERCENARY   The money was good.

DOMINATRIX I would find the man for him no matter what
               I had to go through.
               I wanted to please him, more than that,
               I wanted to help him,
               more than that I wanted
               to be the one to release him
               from a pain no one else was capable of
               releasing him from.
               I knew exactly how he felt,
               why he had made that decision,
               how important it was for him to have total
               control of the way he went.

MERCENARY   'The boy will be naked,' she said,
               and 'I'll be by his side.'

DOMINATRIX 'All you'll have to do is bring him off
               with one hand and slowly,
               gently but firmly squeeze the life out of him
               with the other,
               holding him by the throat tighter and tighter,
               looking at his eyes all the while.
               No words. No let up. All the way.'

MERCENARY   'I'm no fucking queer,' I said.

DOMINATRIX 'You don't have to be, darling, it's a job.'

MERCENARY She said. I thought about it and decided to take it.
But while I was doing it, there was something in
that boy's eyes that freaked me out.
He had them fixed on me in a way that…
they pierced right through me. *(Beat.)* He looked
at me in a way that made me feel all shaky,
kind of scared. Now, that's well unlike me.
I'd been in some deep shit in my life,
but I'd never felt scared.
Not until then. I've got to finish this job,
I told myself.
I've got to finish it!

PRIEST I dreamed of him every night after he left.
In the dreams, I knew exactly
what he was going through.
But I couldn't stop him.

MERCENARY Something about that boy's face I'd not seen
before. Anywhere.
On anyone. Except perhaps. *(Beat.)*
I did have a son once.
(Pause.) I…was slapping his mum around,
you know, the usual,
not very hard or anything, just had a pint too
many, and this little kid comes and stands right
in front of me and stares me in the face.
I was gobsmacked. I had to stop, I'm telling you
I had to stop hitting his mum and I started with him.
The little sod standing up to *me. (Pause.)*
I lashed out, then I collapsed.
I had quite a bit to be honest.
His mum grabbed him, run out the door and…
that was it.
Never saw them again. Lost all trace of them…

DOMINATRIX The kind of pleasure
you can only experience
once in your life
is worth dying for.

MERCENARY   Well, that boy's eyes reminded me of my son
looking at me,
only it was a lot more weird than that.
It was like he was taking me with him.
It was like it was my life
I was squeezing out of him.
Now I've killed quite a few fuckers in my time
but I'd never felt anything like that.
(Beat.) I did finish the job all right but
I don't want another job like it. Ever.

PRIEST   The dreams continued after his death.
Only they became more intense.
They were no longer dreams.
They were experiences
between waking and dreaming realities.
Three of them. The first two were mere
preparations for the third.
I knew then he had come back to claim
what was his by rights... Me.
But I wasn't ready... It was like this:

I'm lying down on a single bed, eyes wide open...
I'm staring at the blank wall.
There I suddenly see him.
Full of brilliant white light.
Smiling at me, beckoning me...
We stretch our hands, they touch...
He gently lies beside me...
face to face, in silence...
I'm as close to heaven as you can be...
I'm getting higher and higher...
I lose all sense of time *and* space ...

Then something shifts.
I can't breath. I'm choking.
I realize there is no air in that space
and if I stay any longer, I'll die.
Literally. Aris is calmly waiting...
for me to stop breathing. *(Pause.)*

It was like fighting a useless battle.
Yet something inside you,
survival instinct I suppose, urges you on.
Urges you on to fight. And you fight.
And I fought. I fought to start breathing again,
to come back to *this* reality, to life.
And I did... Without him...
I should have let go... Stayed together...

DOMINATRIX Too late now...

Silence.

PRIEST *(Resolutely.)* I pushed him to it. There is no
doubt about it. I'm to blame!

VOICE OVER May I point out again that
whenever there is resistance,
regrets persist and guilt refuses to be erased,
higher dosages become necessary,
running the risk of fatal consequences...

PRIEST I should rot in jail!

VOICE OVER May I repeat: guilt must be absolutely eliminated!
However, a higher dose may prove fatal...

PRIEST *(Quietly.)* Do whatever needs to be done...
punish me, please, release me!

Silence.

*The MERCENARY and the DOMINATRIX look at the PRIEST with
a momentary sympathy but quickly revert to self-survival. The
DOMINATRIX, MERCENARY & BODYBUILDER create gradually
another triptych. The PRIEST and the BODYBUILDER form a
diptych. The ANOREXIC stands alone.*

MERCENARY It was a job. I couldn't refuse.

DOMINATRIX I did what I did out of love.

MERCENARY I reckon I won't do any more contract work.
(Beat.)

As a matter of fact, I'm thinking of
giving this line of work a bit of a break.

ANOREXIC I started eating again after it was all over.
getting there... I'm free really...strong...
Choc choc chunk chunk
cookies, cookies.

BODYGUARD I mean – how do you get close
without losing yourself?
Can you learn that sort of thing?
Is it too late?

MERCENARY Never too late, mate,
never too late to change course,
if it's to avoid a crash.

DOMINATRIX Is there a more generous act, I ask you,
than risking everything you've got,
so that you give the ultimate gift to your lover?
Is there?

*Lights diminishing on each character's face and slowly fading,
while ARIS is silently watching them.*

The End.

Nina Rapi's plays include: *Angelstate, Wild Beats/ Agries Notes, Kiss the Shadow, Reasons to Hide, Edgewise/Akrovasia, Lovers, Dreamhouse, Dance of Guns,* and *Ithaka,* as well as a number of shorts. Her plays have been produced or presented at venues such as: Southbank Centre, Soho Theatre studio, Lyric studio, Tristan Bates, ICA, Riverside studios, Gielgud Theatre (London), National Theatre, Theatro Technis, Theatro Empros, Aggelon Vima, Bib (Greece), India (Pirani), and Estaca Zero Teatro, Porto, Portugal. She is the recipient of two Arts Council writing awards, a group award (Raymond Williams), a Best Play Award (BITS Festival, India), and High Recommendation (Future Perfect competition). She has also been shortlisted in numerous competitions, including BBC international short story competition.

Essays on her work by other writers and essays by her on aesthetics and sexuality have been published by Cambridge University Press, Routledge, Mimesis Edizioni, Cambridge Scholars Press, Harwood Academic Press, among others. She has taught Creative Writing at the Universities of London and Greenwich for many years. She is also the founding Editor of Brand Literary Magazine. Her latest collection of short stories *State of Fugue/Katastasi Fougas* was published in 2014 (Kedros, Athens). Also in 2014, her opera libretto *Raven* (composer K. Kritsotakis) was performed at Onassis Cultural Centre, S.G.T., Athens.

WOLFGANG
by Yannis Mavritsakis

Translated by Christina Polyhroniou

The Tyranny of Purity

In her hair, in her armpits,
Between her legs, madness nestles that will destroy you...

The second play of Yannis Mavritsakis was inspired by a real event which shocked the public opinion in summer 2006. Eight years before, a thirty-six-year-old man had kidnapped a ten-year-old girl and held her imprisoned in his home in an Austrian suburb, hiding her for most of the time in a five-square-meter basement. This act was revealed when the girl managed to escape, at the age of eighteen. That same evening the man committed suicide by throwing himself on the railway tracks. In a message, the girl stated: "He was part of my life; in a way I am mourning for him."

At the Antipodes of the Media Ethics

By contrast to the mass media, which faced the event as an individual case arousing voyeuristic morbidity and lust, Yannis Mavritsakis's text is interested in discerning the everyday behind the exceptional, the human behind the inhuman, the archetypal motivation behind crime and extremity. This is why he focuses less on events and more on their psychic echo. The plotline develops in a slow rhythm, letting the inner action in the characters' fantasy to become obvious through their meticulous dialogical debate. Wolfgang and Fabienne as much as the Neighbour, the Mother, the Friend and the Woman are basically realistic characters but they also function as symbolic figures of a frightening world, orchestrated by the ghost of the Father. The elements that form the scenic background – the garden, the car, the basement: all remnants of a past peaceful life – play no other role than to strengthen the feeling of nightmare in the soul of people.

It is easy to recognize all these characters: the authoritarian father, the hysterical mother, the nouveau-riche antagonistic neighbour. Their unstable environment and their motivation – stark antagonism but also painful insecurity and jealousy mixed with fear for the other – could well be ours. In this sense, the contemporary conception of the human in the play does not seem to be that far from its primitive feudal counterpart. This is so not only because Wolfgang imprisons Fabienne. Like the hero himself, his action is the symbolic expression of a civilization which is decaying because of its obsession with ownership. Even if today this obsession seems to refer mainly to the car, the house and generally material possessions rather than the woman or the family (since post-capitalist consumerism also finds expression in the free-of-guilt exchange of erotic partners), Wolfgang emerges – through the girl's kidnapping – as the superego of the western conscience. He demands that civilization "return to its roots," to a morality of utmost simplicity, which, in the play, extends from erotic relations to material goods. But of course, this way of thinking proves equally destructive since it is based on precisely the same ideology as the so-called "pluralistic" morality which it is supposed to fight against.

"Love should be different…," says Wolfgang." You should be able to single someone out… Out of all the rest and stay together for ever."[1] But does this prerogative work both ways? In fact, the subject of this claim is himself exclusively. The *other* is not given any possibility of choice.[2] And of course this is why his preference goes to an underage girl, who has not learned how to choose yet. "Purity" is imposed on her. Absolute devotion springing from the natural need of two people in love becomes a female duty.

War of the Sexes

Monogamy, as Engels claims in *The Origin of the Family, Private Property and the State*, does not enter history as a reconciliation between man and woman. It emerges as the enslavement of one sex by the other, as a war of the sexes, a war unknown to all prehistory.

[1] *Wolfgang*, Scene 8.

[2] *Wolfgang*, Scene 27, "WOLFGANG: Out of all the people I chose you. FABIENNE: Did I choose you? WOLFGANG: You chose me… When you were little."

Similarly, in the play the girl has to bear the tyranny of purity – sometimes with patience, at other times with pure hatred, thus fulfilling the classical scheme of the monogamous relationship. As a guardian of such a tyrannical tradition, Wolfgang tries to ease the contradiction between duty and desire. But the fear of betrayal motivating his action does not derive from the woman's behaviour towards him. It has nothing to do with love, nor with the need for recognition by the loved one – despite the bond he manages to create with his victim. His fear predates this relationship – any relationship. It is a fear rooted in the Male, in the way he conceives himself, as if nothing can threaten his power more than female betrayal. There is just one remedy for this: suppressing the voice of its source. The domination of the male presupposes the gagging of the female.

This is why Fabienne must get isolated since early childhood: Her purity, which is mainly based on her *virginity*, must be preserved so that she can deserve the man who has chosen her. "A virgin body has the freshness of secret springs, the morning bloom of a closed corolla, the orient of the pearl the sun has never caressed. Cave, temple, sanctuary or secret garden: like the child, man is fascinated by these shadowy and closed places never yet touched by animal consciousness [...] It seems to him that he in fact created what he is the only one to grasp and penetrate," as Simone de Beauvoir writes.[3] Finally, is not Wolfgang's obsession the expression of the western man's diachronic fantasy, which is experienced here to the extreme?

A Postmodern Arnolphe

It is to this same theme that Molière's classical comedy *The School for Wives* also turns its focus. Disgusted with the female gender, Arnolphe, the central character who bears the name of deceived husbands (!), adopts a young girl, who also bears a significant name, Agnes. He sends her to a nunnery until her puberty and then he shuts her up in his home under strict supervision for her "education," so that he can later

---

[3] Simone de Beauvoir, *The Second Sex*, (trans.) Constance Borde and Sheila Malovany-Chevalier, Vintage Books, New York 2011, p. 208

marry her. Of course, the theme of the deceived husband has always been a source of inspiration for comedy writers. What distinguishes Molière and gives his play a tragic tone is that his hero is obsessed with the fear of betrayal even before he goes to matrimony. Due to this obsessive idea he builds a completely fantastic plan and when this plan collapses, he too collapses with it.

This is exactly what happens to Wolfgang. There is one vital difference, however, which Mavritsakis has inherited from the pioneers of modern drama and which distinguishes him from the comedy of manners: his hero does not define himself. His act is clearly connected to the social and genealogical circles he belongs to and it surfaces as the unavoidable outcome of a chain of poisoned relationships, of which he too – and despite himself – constitutes a sensitive link. Wolfgang is, therefore, entitled to shutting up Fabienne in the basement but her kidnapping is much more than proleptic by comparison to the imprisonment of Agnes in the house of Arnolphe: It is "therapeutic" because it aims at closing an earlier wound – the Father's pathological jealousy for the Mother.

In this context, Mavritsakis's hero is in no way a scapegoat, a ridiculous social paradox – that of the jealous husband stereotype, which becomes the target of the comedy of manners. On the contrary, he embodies the clearest symptom of a morbid social system, whose every single member has been contaminated by the malady of the male, irrespective of gender. It is disgust that isolates the hero from his environment and makes him contemptuous of "normal life," to the point of fighting it in all possible ways. Wolfgang has not made Fabienne's father or his own family his special target: his target is the "corruption" of the institution of the family in general. Through the underground nest he (as an engineer) has built for Fabienne, he resists the "lie" and the "barbarity" of everyday life.

However, the hero is neither parodied, nor indicted, nor pitied for his action. The author seems to suggest that it would be hypocritical to set up dividing lines between fair and unfair, moral and immoral, right and wrong, in a world where every sense of measure has been lost. This is why he distributes guilt and innocence evenly to all the characters of the play. His language is raw and icy whether he adopts the perspective of the victimizer or the victim.

Dimitra Kondylaki
Dr. of Comparative Literature, Sorbonne, Paris IV

Characters

WOLFGANG

FABIENNE

THE NEIGHBOUR

THE FRIEND

THE MOTHER

THE FATHER'S GHOST

THE WOMAN

THE JEWELLER

1

WOLFGANG and his NEIGHBOUR up on ladders. Between them a hedge that almost hides the one from the other. They are holding large garden shears. They are trimming the hedge.

NEIGHBOUR
They grow so quickly and you have to cut them back regularly. A little at a time. Otherwise they lose their shape and it's not easy to rectify.

WOLFGANG
Yes. They grow very quickly.

Silence.

NEIGHBOUR
Trimming a hedge requires a certain skill. You mustn't place the shears in too deeply. You might denude it and all the inner branches will show. The little leaves on the surface must be enough to cover the interior. When you see it from the road it should look completely green, and no-one should be able to see what's behind it. And, of course, that's the principal virtue of a hedge. It hides you.

WOLFGANG
Yes. It's a kind of protection.

NEIGHBOUR
Not that they can stop a burglar...but they keep out indiscreet eyes.

Silence.

And of course the art is getting it even...not a bit higher there, a bit lower here... It has to look as if you've cut it with a knife. That's where the beauty lies.

WOLFGANG
Yours are just like that. As if you've cut them with a knife.

NEIGHBOUR
Yours too...they're not bad. An experienced eye can discern a slight unsteadiness, but on the whole they're not too bad.

WOLFGANG
Not like yours though.

NEIGHBOUR
Yes, it's true that mine are the best on the block. Perhaps even the best in the area. I've seen how passersby look at them. Strangers with admiration and neighbours with envy.

Silence.

WOLFGANG
I wouldn't like to be envied.

NEIGHBOUR
First time I've heard anyone say that. I thought everyone liked to be envied.

WOLFGANG
I don't.

NEIGHBOUR
It's a pleasure... To be envied for what you are... Or for something you have...

WOLFGANG
I wouldn't like it. It would worry me.

NEIGHBOUR
I'm not at all worried.

Silence.

Come and eat with us one Sunday. My wife makes a great pork dish with plums.

WOLFGANG
Thank you.

NEIGHBOUR
We've been neighbours for so many years, my wife says, only a few shrubs separate us and yet we've never visited each others' houses. Bring your girlfriend too...

WOLFGANG
I haven't got a girlfriend. No-one steady.

NEIGHBOUR
I understand… That doesn't change anything. The invitation stands.

Silence.

You're quite a loner for a bachelor. I've never happened to see people coming and going from your house.

WOLFGANG
I prefer a quiet life.

NEIGHBOUR
I haven't ever seen any ladies either… Except for your mother… I suppose you have visitors late at night, when us family men are getting ready for bed.

Silence.

And you never married…

WOLFGANG
No.

NEIGHBOUR
At your age you should. Marriage helps a man mature.

Silence.

We're a happy family. We have our little problems, but we're happy. I've got a good business, my wife works too and brings in extra money, Fabienne is doing well at school… On Sundays, our friends come round, we watch football on TV Sport, the women chat, the children play in the garden. It's a good life.

Silence.

If you ever need a bouquet of flowers and can't find a florist open, come and pick some from our garden. We have a huge variety, summer and winter. My wife never picks them. She says she doesn't like decorating the house with dead flowers.

Silence.

That's it... Now it's perfect. At least on my side. How is it on yours?

WOLFGANG
On my side too. I think it's fine.

2

WOLFGANG and his FRIEND. They're repairing the car.

FRIEND
Why don't you get a new one? You're making enough money now.

WOLFGANG
I like this one.

FRIEND
If you think about the money you spend on the parts...

WOLFGANG
It's not about money. I like it.

FRIEND
When your father bought it, it was in tip-top condition...
but now...

WOLFGANG
Now too, it's fine.

FRIEND
I'd be ashamed to drive around in a car like this.

WOLFGANG
Why?

FRIEND
It's degrading... Isn't it? Not even the last immigrant off the boat... Even immigrants drive better cars than this now.

WOLFGANG
Everyone has the right to drive whatever car they like.
What difference does it make?

FRIEND
If it didn't make a difference you'd be wearing your father's shoes too. His suits... His underwear and his pyjamas...

WOLFGANG
He was bigger than me.

FRIEND
Otherwise you'd be wearing them...

WOLFGANG
Wearing his shoes...that would be a bit macabre. The car's different.

FRIEND
It's just as macabre. A twenty-year-old car...

WOLFGANG
Twenty-five year old.

FRIEND
A twenty-five year old car in this suburb... It's weird.

WOLFGANG
No-one has complained.

FRIEND
People here are discreet.

WOLFGANG
In fact, they like it.

FRIEND
Maybe some old man might...but there are no old men in our neighbourhood.

Silence.

Yesterday I was with my girl. She says her friend asks about you all the time.

WOLFGANG
Asks what?

FRIEND
Asks... She wants to know... If you've got a girlfriend, if you like steady relationships, if you've said anything about her...

Silence.

What shall I tell her?

WOLFGANG
Who?

FRIEND
My girl... What shall I tell her to tell her friend?

WOLFGANG
I don't know... I haven't thought about it.

Silence.

FRIEND
We're thinking of going bowling tomorrow. The three of us. Will you come?

WOLFGANG
I've got things to do. If I finish early...

Silence.

FRIEND
She really likes you. You're not exactly her type...but there's something about you she likes, she says.

Silence.

I don't understand women. They reckon they need to have their brains turned on in order to do it... As if they do it with their brains...

Silence.

Bowling... I can't be bothered... But I have to pretend to like it.

WOLFGANG
Why?

FRIEND
Because, like I told you, women's brains get turned on first.
They'll sleep with someone who likes bowling rather than
someone who prefers to sit around drinking beer.

Silence.

Did you tighten it properly?

WOLFGANG
Yes. I think it's tight enough.

FRIEND
Shall I try too?

WOLFGANG
No...you'll get dirty.

FRIEND
I don't mind...

WOLFGANG
It's not necessary. It's tight.

Silence.

Thanks for the help.

FRIEND
Don't mention it. Tomorrow you can treat us to the bowling...

WOLFGANG
I don't know if I'll come...

FRIEND
Think about it... She's a nice girl...

WOLFGANG
I could see that...

FRIEND
Wait till you see her breasts...naked.

WOLFGANG
Have you seen them?

FRIEND
In a photo... She and my girlfriend went on a trip to Italy in the summer. They took loads of photos. In front of ruins, with fountains, with statues... In one of them they posed barebreasted.

WOLFGANG
I've got things to do tomorrow. If I finish early...

3

WOLFGANG with his MOTHER.

MOTHER
What are you digging?

Silence.

Not for planting... You wouldn't be digging so deep.

Silence.

Not to find water either... The public water supply provides enough for your garden.

Silence.

You must do something about this armchair... Or throw it away.

Silence.

Yesterday two men rang my doorbell... Salesmen...from a phone company... They wanted to sell me a subscription. I was frightened when I saw them from the window. They were wearing dark suits and white shirts. They were carrying briefcases. From a distance they looked very... official. As if they represented some government agency... Representatives of the state, I thought, knocking on my door...it can't be anything good... I was so frightened that when I opened the door I couldn't understand what they were saying for a while... I wasn't listening... I was looking at their faces...at their briefcases... I was sure that they were telling me something very bad...that they were hiding something terrifying in their papers... By the time I realised that they were talking about a telephone subscription... my knees had given way... But even then I wasn't sure... Then I noticed their clothes... They didn't fit well, as if they were borrowed... Their shoes were dusty...their collars were loose around their necks...you could easily guess at the dirt underneath... I almost shut the door in their faces. I was so angry. And even after they'd gone, the fear stayed with me... As if they'd brought something unpleasant into the house... I'm still not sure they were really salesmen... Just because they said they were doesn't mean they really were... They may have been just pretending.

Silence.

And I never open the door to strangers... Anyone might do me harm if they want to. Even a child. I always lean over and look through the window.

Silence.

I hope it's not my grave...

Silence.

Eh? Is that it? Are you digging my grave?

WOLFGANG
Your time hasn't come yet. Don't worry.

MOTHER
You don't get advance warning of that.

WOLFGANG
You still have the energy to check up on me. That means your time hasn't come.

MOTHER
I don't check up on you... I come to see if you're all right.

Silence.

No...it's not the armchair... It's my bones creaking...
They've started crumbling...

Silence.

Aren't you going to tell me what you're digging?

WOLFGANG
I'm making a nest.

MOTHER
A nest? Under the ground? What kind of nest is that? For rats?

WOLFGANG
Yes. I'm digging a nest for rats.

MOTHER
Rats have no need of you and your shovel. They manage
perfectly well on their own.

WOLFGANG
The healthy ones do. But there are sick ones too. There are
very old rats, helpless ones, toothless ones, others that the
plough has left disabled... Someone has to help those ones.

Silence.

MOTHER
You've ruined the garden... So many beautiful flowers...

WOLFGANG
You have your own garden. You can plant things.

MOTHER
I can't... I'm an old woman. I've planted lots of flowers in my
life. I can't anymore.

WOLFGANG
You're not old. You pretend to be.

MOTHER
My fingers are swollen... Can't you see?

Silence.

They'll kill me one day… Someone will appear in front of me one day for precisely that reason. To kill me. As long as it happens suddenly and quickly. So I don't have time to see my life flash before my eyes.

4

WOLFGANG and FABIENNE. She's hidden behind the hedge, watching him.

WOLFGANG
Why are you hiding?

FABIENNE
I'm not hiding…

Silence.

WOLFGANG
How was school today?

FABIENNE
Not good.

WOLFGANG
Didn't you do your homework?

FABIENNE
Not because of that.

WOLFGANG
Why?

FABIENNE
Some kids stopped me…when we were coming out of school. They stole my money and my watch.

WOLFGANG
Did you know them?

FABIENNE
No. They were from another neighbourhood.

WOLFGANG
Did they hurt you?

FABIENNE
A bit. When they pulled my hand to get the watch.

WOLFGANG
Did you tell your parents?

FABIENNE
Yes. And they told the police.

WOLFGANG
Were they caught?

FABIENNE
I don't know. I don't care about the money. The watch was a present from Daddy.

WOLFGANG
He'll get you another one.

FABIENNE
I want that one.

WOLFGANG
He'll buy you a better one.

FABIENNE
I want that one. What are you digging?

WOLFGANG
I'm making a shelter.

FABIENNE
In case of war?

WOLFGANG
Yes, in case of war.

FABIENNE
There are no wars anymore.

WOLFGANG
You never know.

Silence.

Will you come and see it?

FABIENNE
When shall I come?

WOLFGANG
When it's finished.

FABIENNE
Will it be nice?

WOLFGANG
Yes, like a normal house. Only it'll be very small.

FABIENNE
Like a toy house...

WOLFGANG
Yes, like a toy house. Will you come and see it?

FABIENNE
When it's finished I'll come.

WOLFGANG
I don't want anyone else to know about it though.

FABIENNE
Why not?

WOLFGANG
A shelter has to be secret. Otherwise it's not a shelter.

FABIENNE
All right. I won't tell.

WOLFGANG
It'll be our secret...

FABIENNE
If there's a war I'll come and hide.

WOLFGANG
Yes, if there's a war you'll come and hide here... Until it's over.

5

WOLFGANG with his FATHER'S GHOST. The car's lights are on.

GHOST
Don't believe her when she says she's afraid. She's not afraid of anyone.

WOLFGANG
I know. I don't believe her.

GHOST
That's how this machine works. She makes you feel sorry for her... She makes you soften, pay attention to her... Then she grabs you by the throat and drinks your blood.

WOLFGANG
She can't do that anymore. She's old now. She's grown cold.

GHOST
Always terrified...with her breasts hanging down to her navel... And underneath she's on fire. What she wouldn't give for someone's saliva on her wrinkled mouth, for a firm caress between her legs. Women have a vacuum there...between their legs, a second stomach under their normal stomach which is never satisfied. Even if they swallow you whole they're still hungry. The hunger never stops. Only in the grave. Only there do they find peace...

Silence.

I built this house with my own hands... Look after it.

WOLFGANG
I'll look after it...

Silence.

GHOST
Don't believe them...

WOLFGANG
She's just a girl...

GHOST
There's always a secret plan behind everything.

WOLFGANG
She's not a woman yet...

GHOST
Even if she's not, she will be. She'll never forgive you your strength. She'll lie in wait. She'll wait for the moment when you show weakness, the moment when you're off guard...to drop the axe on your head. Only then will she be at peace. When she sees your head fall.

WOLFGANG
She's still a girl.

6

WOLFGANG with his MOTHER. WOLFGANG is washing the car.

MOTHER
Your father's two dead dogs are following me. Your father himself. As he was when he was young. With his legs strong. His hair black.

> *Silence.*

> We'd gone on some lovely trips in this car... Most of the time we ended up arguing...but we usually started out well.

> *Silence.*

> That's how it is with most things...they usually start out well.

> *Silence.*

> You keep it in very good condition. Almost as it was when he bought it. Do you wax it? Your father would wax it every now and again.

> *Silence.*

My life has gone by without my understanding...

WOLFGANG
There's nothing about life to understand.

MOTHER
I always told myself...this moment you have to hold on to...
When you grow old you'll have this moment to remember.
I thought it would help me...to have held on to some good
moments. It doesn't help... No moment, however beautiful,
can help.

Silence.

And now why is he following me? What does he want from
me?

Silence.

A pair of sunglasses. They must have been left in the co-
driver's locker. Have you seen them?

WOLFGANG
Yes. They're in there.

MOTHER
They were my favourite pair...

WOLFGANG
Do you want them?

MOTHER
No, I don't need them now... They can stay where they are.

Silence.

Wolfgang... You're my son...

WOLFGANG
I know.

MOTHER
You're so big and strong... I am so weak... And yet...you're my
son...

Silence.

He never believed I was his. I was his alone. I was no-one else's. Even if I emptied my head in front of him so he could see what I was thinking, he still had his doubts. If he could have locked up my mind, he would have done it. But how do you lock up someone's mind. An irrational desire. Destructive. That's how someone is destroyed. When he can't withstand his irrational desires.

Silence.

What do you want with rats? They're not suitable pets. Get a cat or a dog. Rats are dirty animals, they transmit diseases.

WOLFGANG
I'll vaccinate them.

Silence.

MOTHER
When your father first brought me here, the house seemed unreal. The garden was beautifully tended, the woodwork freshly painted, the roof just perfect. As if nothing and no-one had gone near it. Not air, or rain, or people. I turned and looked at him. His black hair frightened me, the way it sat shiny and still.

Silence.

Now all I want is to live a few more days without suffering. But there's always something to worry you. Then it was the lack of love, now it's fear. Of everything. That wooden clock in the kitchen... I remember it from when I was virtually just a girl... It's not a clock anymore. It's a time-bomb. I know that at some point it will explode. I can't know when, but I know it will.

Silence.

No... Don't get a dog... Get a canary. Or even better, a parrot. I saw one a few days ago... One with multi-coloured wings, very impressive, standing motionless, with its claws gripping a plastic branch, right next to a wide open door, without a cage. I asked the shopkeeper...how can you have him free like that...aren't you afraid he'll fly away? The parrot can't go anywhere, madam, we've clipped his wings. All he can do is walk up and down his branch... I've never heard such a thing before... A parrot with clipped wings... It's a sin. Isn't it?

Silence.

I ask myself which of the two is better for the parrot. Living in a cage or not being able to fly again?

Silence.

Come here and keep me company. I miss your company.

WOLFGANG
You're here almost every day.

MOTHER
You're always busy with something.

Silence.

Yes, he loved me too. So much that he would have preferred I didn't exist. That's what he wants. That's why he's following me. Even now that he's no longer alive it upsets him that I continue to exist. If he had a body, he'd strangle me with his bare hands. He wants to see me die, alone and sick. Only then will he be at peace.

7

WOLFGANG and FABIENNE. In the car.

FABIENNE
Nice car.

WOLFGANG
It was my father's.

FABIENNE
Daddy's got a nice car too. I never get into Mummy's...
She drives too fast and I get dizzy.

Silence.

WOLFGANG
How was school today?

FABIENNE
School was OK...

WOLFGANG
What wasn't OK?

FABIENNE
Nothing... I had a fight with Mummy...

WOLFGANG
Why?

FABIENNE
About my room... I don't tidy it...

WOLFGANG
Your mother loves you.

FABIENNE
I know she loves me... Daddy too...but I'd like them to love
me more.

Silence.

WOLFGANG
When I was little, I hid in my father's shelter...

FABIENNE
In the basement?

WOLFGANG
It isn't a basement... It's a shelter. I hid for two whole days.
My parents thought I had got lost in the streets or that
someone had kidnapped me... They never thought of the
shelter.

FABIENNE
Two whole days... Weren't you hungry?

WOLFGANG
I had tinned food and water...

FABIENNE
Didn't you get bored?

WOLFGANG
No. I read my books.

FABIENNE
And then?

WOLFGANG
Then?

FABIENNE
When you came out... What happened? Did they beat you?

WOLFGANG
No. Why would they beat me?

FABIENNE
What did they do?

WOLFGANG
They'd been very frightened... They watched me all the time... they didn't want to lose me again. From that day on they loved me more.

FABIENNE
That's what I want too... For them to love me more.

8

WOLFGANG and a young WOMAN. They are lying on the freshly dug earth. THE WOMAN is naked from the waist up.

WOMAN
Are you sure no-one can see us here?

WOLFGANG
Sure.

Silence.

Have you been with lots of men?

WOMAN
Enough.

WOLFGANG
How many?

WOMAN
I don't know... I don't remember...

Silence.

Does it upset you?

WOLFGANG
No.

WOMAN
Does it please you?

WOLFGANG
It makes no difference.

WOMAN
Why do you ask?

WOLFGANG
Out of curiosity.

Silence.

WOMAN
I was expecting to see you that night... You'd said you would come.

WOLFGANG
I had some work to do... It took longer than I thought it would.

WOMAN
I don't like bowling... I went because of you... I don't even know how to hold the ball...

WOLFGANG
Love should be different.

WOMAN
In what way?

WOLFGANG
You should be able to single someone out... To choose them out of everyone else and be with them forever.

WOMAN
That doesn't happen...

WOLFGANG
It does.

Silence.

WOMAN
Your friend says that you're private.

WOLFGANG
Private?

WOMAN
That you don't open up... That you don't communicate easily... I don't mind... I like private people. There's something to look forward to.

Silence.

Maybe I was wrong... To ask for your phone number... To come here today.

WOLFGANG
You wanted to.

WOMAN
Yes... I thought it would be different... I like you.

WOLFGANG
You don't feel comfortable.

WOMAN
No.

WOLFGANG
With the others?

WOMAN
It's different every time...

WOLFGANG
How is it this time?

WOMAN
Are you sure no-one can see us? I feel embarrassed...

WOLFGANG
I'm sure. There are hedges.

Silence.

WOMAN
Sometimes I don't know how to act... I have my job, my friends...but sometimes I don't know how to act...what to expect...

Silence.

I'd like to see you again...

Silence

Will you call me?

Silence.

It doesn't matter... I don't need to play that game... to be chased after... I'll call you.

9

WOLFGANG on the ground. His MOTHER.

MOTHER
You'll catch a cold... It's damp...

WOLFGANG
I'm not old. My bones can stand it.

MOTHER
I dreamt of you last night... You were small. Not young...
Small... Tiny... I held you in the palm of my hand... You were
saying something but I couldn't hear you. Then you got even
smaller...until you disappeared. I woke up shouting your name.
It wasn't nice.

WOLFGANG
I'm still here. Look...

MOTHER
I see you... Don't go in there. You don't need it. You are big
and strong.

WOLFGANG
It isn't for me.

MOTHER
You'll be swallowed up. You'll become tiny. I don't want to
shout your name and you not to exist.

10

WOLFGANG on the ground. His FATHER'S GHOST.

GHOST
Fight. Not only in a real war. Everywhere. Have you ever been
in a business meeting, at a negotiation table? Have you seen
how they all sit around, with ties or without, how they watch or
don't watch each other, how they calculate their strength, how
they weigh up the opponent, how they lower their eyes ready
to spray their ink at the right moment...how they puff out their

chest to show determination... They fight. Each one in his own way, with the means at his disposal, with whatever nature has given him. One will pounce and thrust the knife into whatever heart or spleen resists him, another circles patiently, another will throw down his arms in a gesture of good will, always keeping a hidden stiletto above his ankle, another pretends to give in to gain time to regroup, another calls for justice, the spirit of peace, the principles that unite people no matter what side they are on. But they all fight. Each one in his own way. Don't ever forget that. Don't be fooled into softening. A man needs to soften, or he may break into a thousand pieces, but don't ever truly soften. Never feel pity. For anyone. Only if you are sure he is dead. Only then can you feel sorry for someone, and even cry for him.

11

FABIENNE.

FABIENNE
When am I going to get out of here?

Silence.

You said it was only for a little while. For a few days. Just to frighten Mummy and Daddy. Like a game.

Silence.

You told me it would be like a game.

Silence.

I'm tired of it.

Silence.

I want to go home. To my room. This shelter is very dark. There's the lamp-light but it's dark.

Silence.

I want to look out the window. There's no window here.

Silence.

I've read all the books you brought me. I've re-read them. I want to go outside, to see my friends, Daddy and Mummy. They'll be worried. They may even die of worry, I don't want anything bad to happen to them, I love them. You said it was just for a little while, to frighten them a bit. I don't want anything bad to happen to them.

Silence.

When is this game going to stop?

Silence.

Answer me.

12

WOLFGANG on the ground.

WOLFGANG
I chose you. Out of all people I chose you. You'll stay hidden there. You're not in danger now. You're protected and safe. No-one can touch you. You'll remain pure. No matter how many years go by. You'll never grow old. Even when you've become a woman, you'll still be a girl. Until you become a part of me. Until nothing can separate us.

13

FABIENNE.

FABIENNE
Let me out or I'll start to scream.

Silence.

My parents are sleeping next door. They'll hear me.

Silence.

However deep in the earth you've hidden me, they'll hear. They'll wake up.

Silence.

My father will grab you by the throat. He'll throw you off the roof.

Silence.

Let me out. I'm drowning.

Silence.

It's not a game. It's a deep well. My lungs have filled with water.

14

WOLFGANG and THE JEWELLER. At THE JEWELLER's feet there's a dog sleeping.

WOLFGANG
Nice dog.

JEWELLER
It's not a dog. It's my wife.

Silence.

I look after it and love it as if it was my wife. Do you want silver, gold or platinum wedding rings?

WOLFGANG
Platinum.

JEWELLER
The women I had before would have left me without a second thought. It would have been enough for someone better than me to look at them. There's always someone better… What do you think of these?

Silence.

I'll show you something else… For this dog, there's no-one but me. He follows me everywhere, at night he curls up at the foot of the bed, he keeps me company. He'll never betray me. These?

Silence.

Something else then... Since this dog found me, no woman has ever entered my house. Now it's enough for me to touch the hands of the women who come in to try on rings. What do you think?

WOLFGANG
They're beautiful.

JEWELLER
The lady will have to try on hers...

WOLFGANG
She's not a lady. Not yet.

JEWELLER
She has to try it on...

WOLFGANG
It will fit. Engrave our names on them.

JEWELLER
The initials?

WOLFGANG
Not the initials. The whole names. Wolfgang and Fabienne.

JEWELLER
There's a small charge...

WOLFGANG
On mine engrave Fabienne and on hers engrave Wolfgang.

JEWELLER
You must be very close...

WOLFGANG
We'll be together forever.

15

WOLFGANG with THE NEIGHBOUR. They are trimming the hedge.

NEIGHBOUR
I've neglected it lately and it's lost its shape. It's hard work to get it back.

Silence.

They've stopped looking.

Silence.

I sit at the window sometimes. I hide behind the curtains and watch the passers-by. They've stopped looking at the garden.

Silence.

I still do the same things. I go to work every day. And so does my wife. Our friends still come over on Sundays, we watch football on TV Sport, the women chat in the kitchen.

Silence.

I believe she'll come back. I'll open the door one day and find her sleeping in her room.

Silence.

At night, my wife gets out of bed and leaves the room. I don't know where she goes. I don't ask her.

Silence.

One has to be strong. One has to be able to carry on.

Silence.

In the beginning, everyone looked at us pityingly. I've never liked being pitied by others, but when you're suffering even that is something. It means that others are thinking about you. That there's somewhere to direct your sorrow. Not anymore. Time's gone by, so many months, and people are tired of being compassionate. Now I see fear in their eyes…fear that my sorrow is still alive and I'll oblige them to listen to me again, now that their curiosity has been exhausted.

Silence.

I'm afraid my wife will leave me. Not necessarily for someone else. Because she doesn't want to remember any longer.

Silence.

Thank you.

Silence.

You're the only one who listens to me patiently and isn't in a hurry to change the subject.

Silence.

You always need neighbours. Even more than friends. I'd heard it said. Now I understand it.

Silence.

Come over and eat with us one Sunday. You never came again. Fabienne liked you. She really liked the watch you bought her. Perhaps even more than mine. She always wore it and showed it to her friends.

Silence.

The nights when I don't sleep, I hear her voice. It pierces the closed windows. I hear her laboured breathing on the stairs. I can't be wrong. She's alive. She'll come back.

Silence.

What do you think? It's a bit better than it was. Isn't it?

16

WOLFGANG with THE WOMAN. They are lying on the ground. No nakedness.

WOLFGANG
I don't want you to come again. Today is the last time.

Silence.

You'll find someone else... Someone better.

Silence.

WOMAN
I was wrong to show you that I need you.

Silence.

It doesn't matter that there were many. None of them left me with anything. Just a few moments preparing the way for the next few, but that isn't enough for me. You always need something more. Something you can find yourself in.

Silence.

I thought my life had changed...

Silence.

The day you came to my house... I started cleaning early. I wanted you to like it. The cover on the sofa was old and worn. I wondered if you would think of all the others who had sat on it. I rushed around till the last minute, looking for a new one. I wanted everything to be new.

Silence.

I've grown used to you... Every day, when I finished work, I didn't feel tired. Because I thought we might see each other. But even when we didn't meet, the evenings went by more easily. I had the next day to look forward to.

Silence.

You may be making a mistake. It may be a momentary decision and tomorrow morning everything may be back in place.

17

FABIENNE dressed in white. She's holding a small bouquet of flowers. WOLFGANG is exchanging the rings.

FABIENNE
It falls off...

WOLFGANG
You can wear it around your neck for a while... Until your hands get bigger.

Silence.

Now we're married...

Silence.

We're going to be happy...

FABIENNE
You're going to be happy.

Silence.

That wasn't a wedding... You should have invited Mummy and Daddy...

WOLFGANG
Why don't you believe me?

FABIENNE
Because I don't believe you...

WOLFGANG
I'm telling the truth.

Silence.

FABIENNE
Tell me how it happened...

WOLFGANG
I told you.

FABIENNE
Tell me again.

Silence.

WOLFGANG
They were outside...in the garden.

FABIENNE
In what part of the garden?

WOLFGANG
In the front.

FABIENNE
Last time you told me they were at the side...

WOLFGANG
At the side... They were digging... They were planting seeds...

FABIENNE
You didn't tell me about the seeds...

WOLFGANG
That's why they were digging... To plant seeds...

FABIENNE
What kind of seeds?

WOLFGANG
I don't know... I was standing at a distance.

FABIENNE
Lies... My father never planted seeds... Only Mummy...

WOLFGANG
He was helping her with the digging...

FABIENNE
What were they wearing?

WOLFGANG
I don't remember... I didn't notice...

FABIENNE
You're telling lies... Lies...

WOLFGANG
They were wearing... Your mother a blue dress... Your father something grey...

FABIENNE
More lies... My mother had a pair of trousers for the garden...

WOLFGANG
She was wearing blue trousers...

FABIENNE
You killed them...

WOLFGANG
They were killed in front of my eyes... While they were out in the garden... They were planting seeds...

FABIENNE
Why weren't you killed?

WOLFGANG
I ran away at the last minute... I hid in here... I shouted to them but they didn't hear...

FABIENNE
You killed them...

WOLFGANG
I wouldn't even kill a rabbit... There's a war going on outside...

FABIENNE
What war? Why don't you tell me? Who is fighting?

WOLFGANG
No-one knows...

FABIENNE
I want to go outside, I want to see what it's like...

WOLFGANG
There's nothing for you to see... Most people have left and those who are still here lock themselves in their houses from early on... No-one goes out at night and they hide the children in the storerooms.

FABIENNE
I hear the children playing in the street... Their voices come through...

WOLFGANG
That what it seems like... No child goes out in the street... They're hidden in storerooms... You're lucky to have your own shelter...

FABIENNE
Better a storeroom...

WOLFGANG
Now we're married. You're my wife.

Silence.

FABIENNE
Since we're married we have to go on a trip. Let's get out of here secretly and go on a trip.

WOLFGANG
They've closed the borders... There are soldiers keeping guard everywhere.

FABIENNE
Why do you go outside? Why don't they catch you?

WOLFGANG
I'm in danger... Every day I face danger for you... So you can have food and clothes...

FABIENNE
What use are the clothes... No-one sees them...

WOLFGANG
Be patient until the war is over... Then we'll go out together, everyone will look at us...

FABIENNE
I'm scared...

WOLFGANG
What are you scared of?

FABIENNE
That you're lying to me... If you're lying to me...

WOLFGANG
What?

FABIENNE
Nothing... I'll be patient... I'll wait... Until it's over...

18

WOLFGANG and his MOTHER. WOLFGANG is planting.

MOTHER
Today I didn't take the metro. I didn't want to bury myself
under ground again... To be squashed in with all those
strangers... I called a taxi. We got here quite quickly... Not
through the centre... We took the ring road... We went over
the new bridge... It's already old... A car had crashed into
the rails. The driver was lying in the road... I saw him... His
neck was broken... He was bleeding badly... He was having
spasms... His eyes open... He was looking at us watching
him... He knew he wouldn't be with us long... He was looking
at us in a way...as if it all seemed unreal... As if he couldn't
believe what was happening to him...that we would go on
while he wouldn't... I'd never seen anything like that before.

Silence.

Your garden is looking lovely... And you are looking good
too... You seem younger...

Silence.

Only you've become even more quiet... Now you hardly
speak to me at all. I feel even more of an intruder.

Silence.

Tell me it's not so. Tell me that you are still Wolfgang…

WOLFGANG
Yes. I am.

Silence.

MOTHER
I'm not going over that bridge again… Metro is better…

Silence.

What are you hiding in the basement of your house?

Silence.

I know you're hiding someone. I wake up suddenly in the middle of the night. In my sleep I hear someone beating on the walls…

Silence.

Tell me… I am your mother. You can fool everyone, but not your mother. You are my son, I gave birth to you, I hear your thoughts.

Silence.

Tell me… I won't tell… Anyone…

Silence.

Tell me who you're hiding… That girl who was lost?… Are you hiding the girl who was lost?…

WOLFGANG
I'm not hiding anyone.

MOTHER
I won't tell a soul…

WOLFGANG
I'm not hiding anyone.

Silence.

I don't want you to come here again.

19

FABIENNE

FABIENNE
No-one will hear me. Ever. However much I shout. Everyone's carrying on as if nothing's changed. They go to work, they go walking, they joke. I hear their footsteps coming and going, they have their lives. They cook, they eat, they talk on the telephone, they drive their cars. In the evenings they meet somewhere, they eat again, they talk again, then they get sleepy, they go to bed, they get up the next morning. I never get sleepy. I just get tired of waiting, whether standing up or lying down, in the same bed, with the same colours, the same smells and the hum of their lives. I've been planted. My hands are getting longer, I'm growing shoots, my hair is standing on end, trying to reach the air, pushing... I'm going to rot. My eyes have grown dangerously big. They're looking at you. I watch your movements. The way you arrive outside the house, the way you open the garage door, the way you lock that horrible car of your father's, then at the entrance, at the stairs that lead to the bedrooms, to the toilet, the way you contentedly empty yourself, the way you pull up your trousers, the way you wash your hands, look at yourself in the mirror, content again that you're you, that you've locked someone in to wait for you, that you'll show your tenderness again with a little gift, a book, a hair-brush, so I can brush my hair for you, so you can come and see me, see how I've grown, pale, with my legs trembling, with a gift, with food on a tray, let's see how the little one's grown, making sure they're not looking, opening the trapdoor carefully...

Silence.

I'll kill you. Me, with my little hands. Next time I hear you coming down the stairs, I'll become invisible, I'll stand behind you, I'll grab the fork from the tray, the tins of food will spill at your feet, the fork will be impaled in your head, you'll run around with the fork in your head, blinded, you'll crash about the way I crash into the walls, until you are completely emptied out, until there's nothing left of you at all.

20

WOLFGANG with his FRIEND. WOLFGANG is changing the windscreen-wipers of the car.

FRIEND
You don't mind that I turned up without calling... Do you?

Silence.

You should have told me you needed new windscreen-wipers... I could have got them at half price...

Silence.

Yesterday we went to the cinema... Your girlfriend came with us...

WOLFGANG
She isn't my girlfriend.

FRIEND
Your ex... I don't even remember the film we saw... I fell asleep in my seat... The only thing I wanted to do after a hard day's work, was to grab a beer and lie back on the sofa... But you know what women are like... If you don't take them to the cinema now and again...they go crazy...

Silence.

She's miserable... She is still hoping... She thinks that if she doesn't call you, you'll call her. That you'll realise you made a mistake and ask her forgiveness. She'll forgive you and then you'll be together again. That's what she is expecting.

Silence.

Shall I help you?

WOLFGANG
I can manage.

FRIEND
I know you can... Just so I am not sitting around watching...

Silence.

I tell everyone... My friend Wolfgang, I say...can do anything... He can fix everything from a chair to a satellite...

Silence.

And we've known each other a long time... Ever since I opened the garage.

Silence.

I remember you bringing in your father's car... I hadn't seen a car like that in a long time...

Silence.

Yesterday when we went to the cinema... I didn't fall asleep. I just said that. I sat there for the whole two hours with my eyes open. I was looking...but I just didn't see anything. As if the system was blocked. I just remember a hand at some point... I don't know if it was in the film or if I imagined it...a hand that came towards me and then moved back again and then towards me again, as if it was hitting me on the head and backing away. That happened a few times, then the hand disappeared, I couldn't see it, but the head-tapping continued, nothing too hard, like a friendly tap, but it made me dizzy, I felt like throwing up the popcorn and everything else I'd eaten the previous day, but I couldn't get out, we were in the middle of the row, so many people, how could I step over all those feet, I gripped the seat very hard, I held my head steady and tried to look straight ahead, at a specific point, but I couldn't find a specific point, as if there was nothing in front of me, nothing that I could look at...

Silence.

Let's go out some time... Not with women... Just the two
of us... Let's go for a beer... Eh? What do you say?

WOLFGANG
Yes. Let's.

FRIEND
What about tomorrow?

WOLFGANG
Not tomorrow. I've got things to do.

FRIEND
Like what?

WOLFGANG
In the house. I'm fixing the floor.

FRIEND
Shall I come and help you?

WOLFGANG
No. It's not necessary.

FRIEND
For the company...

WOLFGANG
It's not necessary.

FRIEND
We'll have a few beers...

WOLFGANG
Better not.

21

WOLFGANG and FABIENNE.

FABIENNE
What's the news from the war?

WOLFGANG
It's spreading... It's spread to neighbouring countries.

FABIENNE
And what's the prediction? When will it stop?

WOLFGANG
No-one can say. But it won't be soon.

FABIENNE
I've never understood who we're fighting...

WOLFGANG
It's not one enemy... It's many.

FABIENNE
Tell me about all those many... I want to know.

WOLFGANG
You're still too young.

FABIENNE
I'm not... I've grown up. Look... The shoes that I was wearing when you brought me here... They don't fit...

WOLFGANG
I bought you new ones...

FABIENNE
I didn't say it for that...

WOLFGANG
You have everything. You have clothes, books, toys, a bed and your desk. I've changed the hatch, I've fixed the stairs and the wooden floor. You're protected and safe.

FABIENNE
I know... You take care of me...

Silence.

You always come here freshly bathed and clean... Your hair smells nice.

WOLFGANG
I do it for you...

FABIENNE
If only I had a bathtub... I'd soak in the hot water until I fell asleep...

WOLFGANG
You have hot water...

FABIENNE
I'm talking about a bathtub... I wash standing up...

WOLFGANG
Be patient... Later on, we'll both be getting into the bathtub.

Silence.

Come here... I want to kiss you...

FABIENNE
Not again... I'm too young...

WOLFGANG
No, you're not... You've grown up... I want to kiss you...

FABIENNE
If I've grown up, then tell me about the enemies... Tell me who they are...

WOLFGANG
You have to listen to what I say...

FABIENNE
I do listen...

WOLFGANG
You have to do what I say. It's the only way I can be happy...

FABIENNE
Bit by bit... I am still young... I'll learn.

WOLFGANG
It's the only way we can be happy...

FABIENNE
Bit by bit… I'll learn.

Silence.

WOLFGANG
I'm not going to bring you food tonight. You'll go hungry.

FABIENNE
Don't go yet… I'm on my own all day.

WOLFGANG
I'm outside fighting…

FABIENNE
I know… Stay a bit longer…

WOLFGANG
You should be doing your lessons…

FABIENNE
I did them…

WOLFGANG
Say you're sorry.

FABIENNE
For what?

WOLFGANG
Say you're sorry…

FABIENNE
For what?

WOLFGANG
Say you're sorry.

Silence.

FABIENNE
I'm sorry.

Silence.

WOLFGANG
Don't be afraid. I love you... If you're quiet and good I'll always love you. I'll take care of you... I'll be the best and strongest man in the world if you're quiet and good...

22

WOLFGANG and THE JEWELLER. The dog is sleeping at THE JEWELLER's feet.

WOLFGANG
It's for our wedding anniversary.

JEWELLER
So...something good...

WOLFGANG
Yes, something good.

JEWELLER
Gold or platinum?

WOLFGANG
Platinum.

JEWELLER
My wife prefered silver. It suited her personality better.

WOLFGANG
What personality?

JEWELLER
Easy... She liked everyone... A necklace? It will look good with her long neck... Or perhaps a brooch?

WOLFGANG
Not a brooch...

JEWELLER
I agree... I wouldn't buy her a brooch ... A brooch can easily become a weapon in her hands... A bracelet then...

WOLFGANG
Yes, a bracelet.

JEWELLER
With her name engraved...

WOLFGANG
Engrave both names.

JEWELLER
There will be a small charge...

WOLFGANG
Wolfgang and Fabienne.

JEWELLER
How many years are you celebrating?

WOLFGANG
Three.

JEWELLER
I lived for many years with my wife... Almost all my life... I got to know your mother well... I built this house with my own hands, Wolfgang... I told you to guard it well and you brought me the rat to gnaw its foundations... She will destroy you... In her hair, in her armpits, between her legs, nestles the madness that will destroy you... She sleeps and wakes with the same thought... To take you to the heights... To push you with her own hands so that you fall.... She wants to see you fall... You are falling, Wolfgang... You are falling... I'll hold you...

23

FABIENNE and the Object.

FABIENNE
What can you do? Show me.

    Silence.

    Can you stay up in the air?

    Silence.

    Give off light?

Silence.

Open a hole in the roof? Can you?

Silence.

In the floor?

Silence.

Show me... Whatever you think...

Silence.

Is there something you know? Do you have knowledge? Secret knowledge which you've come to bring me in particular?

Silence.

How old are you? What's your age? Everything has a certain age...

Silence.

What's mine? Do you know? He says fifteen... I say fifty... What do you say?

Silence.

I am well preserved for fifty...eh?

Silence.

Where have you come from? Did someone send you?

Silence.

Are you looking at me? Do you have eyes?

Silence.

Ears? Can you hear me?

Silence.

You definitely don't have a mouth...

Silence.

Why did you come? If you can't do anything for me...
then why did you come? To visit?

Silence.

Can you leave now, please? Go away... I want to be
alone... I have to think. What's the time? It's ten in the
morning. There are twelve more hours till ten at night,
when I'll go to sleep. Twelve hours to think.

Silence.

Can you at least give me some information? Somehow...
What are they doing out there, do you know? Who is
winning? Have many died? Give me a picture... I'm lucky.
I have my nest, they won't kill me. You? Have you died
perhaps? Is that why you've come? Do you want to stay with
me? Are you afraid? If he sees you he'll throw you out. He's
not a bad person, he'll do it for me. Because the nest is mine,
he made it for me. So they wouldn't kill me. If he doesn't find
you, you can stay, I won't say anything. You don't take up
any room. You don't ask for anything. You can stay, don't be
scared. We're safe here. Keep quiet and keep me company.
I want to think. I'll think and you'll keep me company.

Silence.

Now I'm thinking about our garden... Mummy and Daddy.
They've died but I think of them. Mummy is taking care of
our flowers. We have lots of flowers, summer and winter.
Dad trims the hedges. It's a sunny day, Mummy is wearing
her hat and gloves so she won't spoil her hands. She has
nice hands, soft. I am coming back from school, she calls
to me to take off my shoes, not to drag dirt into the house.
No, that's not right... Since Daddy's home it's Sunday and I
don't have school... I'm coming back from a friend's house.
I was at my friend's house, down the road... They have a
beautiful house too, with a big garden like ours. We sat in
the garden and talked. About boys... Who we like, what he
said to us...

Silence.

Where do all these things go? Do you know? The
pictures... Where do they end up? Do you know?

Silence.

There's a hole that swallows them all up. They're there,
inside that hole, swirling around all time with other
pictures, ones I don't know, all the pictures swirling around
in that hole, they can't get out, the hole is closed on all
sides, they swirl around, there's no way out, there's nowhere
for them to escape through, if you enter there then there's
no way out, they just swirl around for ever, and new pictures
keep falling in, they get mixed up with the old ones, pictures
unfamiliar to each other, side by side, a snail with Daddy's
boots, the street in front of our school with an aeroplane,
someone who's scratching his nose with someone smiling
at the greengrocer's wife, Mummy's cigarettes and the
television, the doctor's tongue-holder, the sun, all swirling
around in the same hole which can contain even more,
which can contain everything, with no way out, if you enter
there's no way out, all the pictures together, all mixed up
together, they don't change, they stay exactly the same,
they don't grow old, the pictures don't grow old, they don't
die, they stay exactly the way they were, and new ones keep
arriving, they fall in and swirl around with the earlier ones,
all the earlier ones, without end.

Silence.

I can't remember her... My friend...what she was like...
Mummy and Daddy either... I can't remember their faces...
I remember the gloves, the hat, the garden shears,
but I can't remember their faces... They've died. Not
their pictures... Their pictures are in the hole... They
themselves... They've died.

24

WOLFGANG with THE NEIGHBOUR. WOLFGANG is trimming the hedge. THE NEIGHBOUR is holding a suitcase.

NEIGHBOUR
Now it's all yours... You can give it any shape you want...

WOLFGANG
I'll keep it just as you had it. As if cut with a knife.

NEIGHBOUR
You've improved a lot... You've become better than me...

WOLFGANG
I'm learning...

Silence.

NEIGHBOUR
The house hasn't been sold yet... But I can't wait any longer.

Silence.

I've taken an apartment in the centre... Quite a small apartment...but it's big enough for one person... I'll invite you over for a meal some time... No pork and plum dish... We'll order something in.

Silence.

Luckily my wife moved to another city...so it's less likely that we'll run into each other by chance.

Silence.

Yesterday I was packing up the last few things and I found something of yours... A drawing of Fabienne's... She'd made it when she was still very small... 'Mr. Wolfgang watches' she called it... It looks like a dog or a wolf hidden behind a hedge... I suppose she was afraid of you when she was little...

WOLFGANG
The drawing is not of me.

NEIGHBOUR
I thought of you immediately... But maybe I made a mistake.

WOLFGANG
You definitely made a mistake. Fabienne wasn't afraid of me.

NEIGHBOUR
Yes... She wasn't afraid of you... I must have made a mistake.

Silence.

She won't come back. I'm sure of that now. What do you think?

WOLFGANG
Yes. I believe that too. She won't come back.

25

FABIENNE and the Object.

FABIENNE
Are you hungry? If you're hungry I have tinned food from yesterday. I can't eat it. I have a stomach ache. If you have a stomach ache, he says, you should drink water. Water cures everything. I do drink it, but my stomach still hurts. Unless I'm not drinking enough.

Silence.

No, I mustn't complain. About the tinned food. We're lucky to have it. Others have nothing. They're dying in the streets. I wouldn't like to be in their shoes.

Silence.

Even if the war ever finishes, I don't think I'll leave here. Nothing will be like it was and my legs shake. I'll ask him to leave me here, even if I have to eat tinned food, I won't mind. At least I'll have something to eat, and I'll be safe.

The war may finish but that doesn't mean that it's finished for ever. It might start again.

Silence.

These socks don't suit me... He brought them for me yesterday. A present for my birthday. And new underwear. I don't know when I was born. He has a big book where he writes everything. He says I'm a proper woman now, and I have to wear the underwear he brought me. I don't know if I'm a proper woman, but I must be if he says so. His book is never wrong.

Silence.

Do you like it?

Silence.

He wants me to be sweet to him tonight. So he'll be happy. If he's happy I'll be happy too. That's what he says and he's right. I'll be sweet.

Silence.

Please eat that tin of food. If he sees I haven't eaten it he'll be angry. I don't want him to be angry again.

Silence.

It's important to have someone to look after you. Someone who knows everything. Someone who is brave. All these years he's been fighting for me, so I'd have everything I need. He's a good fighter. He's never been wounded. Only once was he wounded in the finger. A bullet skimmed past him.

Silence.

This is our house. This is your house too. Don't you leave either. I hate to think what might happen to you out there. I don't want to lose you. We're bound to each other now.

Silence.

I'm sure he knows about you. He knows everything, so there's no way he doesn't know about you, but it doesn't upset him because you keep me company when he's away. We'll stay here, in our nest. You, me and him. When he comes. Who cares what's happening out there. In here we have nothing to be afraid of.

Silence.

I don't look nice in this underwear. I'm not a woman yet. He says I'm seventeen. I think I'm ten... Not even ten... I think I'm five... Four... I may not even have been born yet...

Silence.

Shall we kill him together? And finally be rid of his filth? He's stuck onto my brain like a leech and he sucks my thoughts. Soon I won't have any thoughts left. Only bones and underwear. Eh? Shall we? It won't be difficult. He's not so strong. Together we could deal with him no problem. And he's never fought in the war. If he had, he would have been killed by now. I bet he's a traitor. He has an agreement with the enemy. That's why we have so many tins of food. Otherwise we would have died like everyone else. I'm not afraid of him. Don't you be afraid of him either. Underneath there's nothing. Do you know how easily someone becomes his own shadow? Eh?... What do you say?... Will you help me? Tell me...will you help me?

Silence.

Then I'll kill you. I'll kill you... I really will... It won't be hard for me to do. At all.

Silence.

Forgive me. I didn't mean to hurt you. I'm so tired. I've dried up. I love you.

26

WOLFGANG.

WOLFGANG
Your car has rotted. I think I'll get someone to remove it. It takes up a lot of space. Fabienne will be born again now. She'll be mine. No-one else will ever touch her. Fabienne will love me for ever. Go to sleep. I'm strong enough now. I've made my garden and I'm guarding the gate. No wolf will get in during the night. The sheep are sleeping quietly. They have nothing to be afraid of. Neither the slaughterhouse, nor a savage dawn with their neck on the butcher's knee. Don't you be afraid either. Go to sleep. We're clean. Me and Fabienne. We're here on our own forever, always loving, without filth and pain. Take it and get out of here. I need space.

27

WOLFGANG and FABIENNE. WOLFGANG is washing the car. FABIENNE is wearing sunglasses.

FABIENNE
I could keep sitting here... In the sun.

    Silence.

    Are we going out?

WOLFGANG
In the car...

FABIENNE
I get dizzy.

WOLFGANG
I'll drive carefully.

FABIENNE
Not because of the car... I'm dizzy.

WOLFGANG
Put on your hat.

FABIENNE
A little longer without a hat...

WOLFGANG
Just a little.

Silence.

FABIENNE
Are they on fire? Our next-door neighbours... Are they on fire?

WOLFGANG
They're having a barbeque. Are you hungry?

FABIENNE
Yes...

WOLFGANG
Me too. We need a good cookbook...

Silence.

FABIENNE
Have you seen them?

WOLFGANG
Who?

FABIENNE
The new neighbours... Have you met them?

WOLFGANG
Yes... I've seen them.

FABIENNE
What are they like?

WOLFGANG
Nice...

FABIENNE
Are they a family?

WOLFGANG
A family.

FABIENNE
Big?

WOLFGANG
A couple and their two children.

FABIENNE
What children?

WOLFGANG
I didn't notice...

FABIENNE
Boys? Girls?

WOLFGANG
A boy and a girl.

FABIENNE
How old?

WOLFGANG
My age...

FABIENNE
Not the couple... The children... Are they young? Older?

WOLFGANG
Young.

FABIENNE
They'll have filled my room with their things...

WOLFGANG
It's their room now.

FABIENNE
It's not theirs... My parents were killed and they stole our house...

WOLFGANG
They didn't steal it... The government gave it to them.

  Silence.

FABIENNE
Is she pretty?

WOLFGANG
Who?

FABIENNE
Their daughter... Is she pretty?

WOLFGANG
I didn't notice...

FABIENNE
You're lying.

WOLFGANG
I don't know... I didn't notice... She's very little.

FABIENNE
So little that you didn't see her?

WOLFGANG
She's a child...

FABIENNE
All the better...

WOLFGANG
Why all the better?

FABIENNE
You like children.

WOLFGANG
What do you mean I like children?

FABIENNE
You like them.

WOLFGANG
I don't mind them.

FABIENNE
You like them.

Silence.

You'll think I'm too old for you now…

WOLFGANG
You aren't old…

FABIENNE
My legs shake….

WOLFGANG
You should walk.

FABIENNE
Where can I walk?

WOLFGANG
Here…in our garden…

FABIENNE
I can't… I can only sit…

WOLFGANG
Sit then.

Silence.

FABIENNE
Will you love me if all I can do is sit?

WOLFGANG
I'll always love you… I chose you.

FABIENNE
Like people choose spinach and potatoes.

WOLFGANG
Out of people…

FABIENNE
Out of children.

WOLFGANG
Out of all people, I chose you.

FABIENNE
Did I choose you?

WOLFGANG
You chose me… When you were little.

FABIENNE
What am I now? Am I old?

WOLFGANG
You are my wife. We love each other.

    Silence.

    Shall we go out? Shopping?

FABIENNE
I can't… I get dizzy.

WOLFGANG
Put on your hat.

FABIENNE
So they don't see me?

WOLFGANG
Because of the sun…

FABIENNE
Because I'm ugly…

WOLFGANG
You are beautiful.

FABIENNE
A beautiful mole.

WOLFGANG
I love you no matter how you look and I will forever.

FABIENNE
Not forever…don't say forever. I want everything to die and to
be re-born… All over again… And then to die again and to be
re-born… Not forever…

Silence.

WOLFGANG
Think about what we need to buy.

Silence.

FABIENNE
Don't ever leave me... I'll break into little pieces.

28

FABIENNE. And later WOLFGANG.

FABIENNE
Wolfgang... Where are you?

Silence.

You said we were going to water the garden... Aren't you coming?

Silence.

Wolfgang... Where are you? Don't hide...

Silence.

Don't do this... It's not nice to hide...

Silence.

Speak to me...

Silence.

You can hear me... I know you can hear me... You hear everything.

Silence.

Are you angry with me? What have I done? I didn't do anything... I am quiet and good... Don't you love me? You know I'm quiet and good...don't you love me?...

Silence.

I didn't do anything... I thought...but I didn't do anything...

Silence.

I only thought... Wolfgang... Forgive me... I only thought...
Where are you? Don't hide... I want to see you... I'm
scared... The garden will swallow me up... I don't want the
garden to swallow me up again... I didn't do anything...
I only thought... Forgive me... I only thought...

Silence.

Wolfgang...

Silence.

My legs won't hold me up... I don't want to lose you...
I love you... I'll love you more...only don't hide... I didn't
do anything bad... I only thought... I only thought...
Wolfgang... I only thought... I thought... I thought... I only
thought... Wolfgang...

WOLFGANG appears. He is wearing a coat and hat.

Why are you dressed like that? You said we were going to
do the watering...

WOLFGANG
Later.

FABIENNE
Are you going out now?

Silence.

Shall we go out?

Silence.

Shall I put my hat on too?

Silence.

And a jacket... I'll bring my jacket...

WOLFGANG
Forget the jacket. First tell me what you thought.

FABIENNE
When? I didn't think anything...

WOLFGANG
You are always thinking.

FABIENNE
There's nothing for me to think...

WOLFGANG
What's in your head, Fabienne? What are you imagining?

Silence.

Give me the picture...

FABIENNE
What picture?

WOLFGANG
The one you're imagining...

Silence.

Don't hide from me... I want you to tell me everything.

FABIENNE
I do tell you everything...

WOLFGANG
Not everything... Now you're keeping things from me...

FABIENNE
I'm not keeping anything from you... I haven't got anything to hide... You can always see me...

WOLFGANG
I see you...

FABIENNE
I can't see you with that hat... It hides your face...

WOLFGANG
Don't you like it hiding my face?

FABIENNE
No... I don't like it... It frightens me...

WOLFGANG
Don't you like that it frightens you?

FABIENNE
No... I don't want it to frighten me...

Silence.

WOLFGANG
Take off your clothes.

FABIENNE
Why should I take them off?... Aren't we going to water the garden?

WOLFGANG
Later. Now, take off your clothes.

FABIENNE
I'm cold...

WOLFGANG
It's not cold...

FABIENNE
You're wearing a coat...

WOLFGANG
Take them off.

FABIENNE
You're wearing a coat and a hat...

WOLFGANG
Take your clothes off...

FABIENNE
Not out here... They'll see me...

WOLFGANG
No-one can see you. Take your clothes off.

Silence.

FABIENNE
I don't want to.

WOLFGANG
Why don't you want to?

FABIENNE
I'm embarrassed...

WOLFGANG
Because of me?

FABIENNE
Not you...

WOLFGANG
What have you done to make you feel embarrassed?

FABIENNE
Nothing...

WOLFGANG
Then don't be embarrassed. Take them off.

Silence.

FABIENNE
If you take yours off too...

WOLFGANG
Afterwards... First you then me.

Silence.

Everything.

FABIENNE
Not everything...

WOLFGANG
Why not everything? You don't have anything to hide...

FABIENNE
I don't have anything to hide...

WOLFGANG
Then everything.

Silence.

So tell me... What did you think about?

Silence.

What was he like, the one you imagined?

Silence.

That man... Did you know him from before?

Silence.

Did you know him or had you seen him somewhere?

Silence.

Had you seen him and remembered him?

Silence.

Every morning when you went to school...was he somewhere watching you? Had that man...spoken to you? Had he stroked your head...your hair? Do you remember his hands stroking your hair?

Silence.

Or perhaps he used to come to your house? That friend of your father's...with the beautiful strong hands... That time he came upon you alone in the kitchen...looking for a clean glass...you couldn't reach the cupboard...you'd climbed on a chair to reach it...he caught you around the waist...he lifted you up with his beautiful strong hands...then he gave you the clean glass... Were you thinking of him?

FABIENNE
I never looked in the cupboard for a clean glass... I wasn't thinking... Let me get dressed...

WOLFGANG
Or perhaps it wasn't one...

Silence.

Tell me, Fabienne... Was it one or many? Don't be ashamed...

Silence.

Tell me what they did to you... The same as I do to you? Did you like it? Or perhaps you did it to them?

Silence.

What did you do to them? How did you do it? Did you bend down or were you on your knees?

FABIENNE
Let me get dressed...

WOLFGANG
Were they all around?... Did you like it? Did you want more... or were you satisfied? Tell me... I don't mind... I want to know... Did you bend down? Did you look them in the eyes? Did you speak to them? What did you say to them? Did you ask for more... Did you want it all?... Tell me... Was it good? Were you happy? Satisfied? Did you want more?

FABIENNE
I want to get dressed...

WOLFGANG
Don't leave me alone... Talk to me... I want to know... Was it better with them or with me? Did you regret it afterwards? Were you ashamed? Do you want it again? How many times? Do you want it again? All the time? With all of those standing around? Do you want it all the time? Have you forgotten me? Did you think of me? Did you remember me? Didn't I exist? Did you forget me? Where was I?

Silence.

Show me... Were you bent down? Or on your knees?
Get on your knees.

FABIENNE
Not on my knees...

WOLFGANG
Bent down?

FABIENNE
My legs shake... They hurt...

WOLFGANG
Get on your knees.

Silence.

Tell me how they came in... One by one or all together?
Standing in a circle or in a line? Did they surprise you? Did
you know them? Did they hurt you? How did they come in?
Did they form a queue? One behind the other? Did they
come to you one after the other? Was it quick or were they
with you for some time? How long with each one? Two
minutes? Five minutes? Ten minutes? A whole day? Where
was I? Did you think of me? That I might have come in?
That I might see you? Where was I at that time? Did you
love me? Me, did you love me at that time? Where was I?
Don't get up... On your knees.

Silence.

Tell me... I want to know... How was it after?

Silence.

Afterwards... How was it? Did you want more? Were
you full? Happy? Whole? How was it? Were you alone?
Unhappy? Did you cry? Were you empty? Tell me. What
exactly? Give me the picture so that I can understand.

FABIENNE
I don't have a picture... Let me get dressed... I don't see
anything...

WOLFGANG
But you did see them... Were they handsome? Big? Strong?
Did they hurt you? Tell me.

FABIENNE
I don't see anything... Only you... Only you... I see...only
you...

WOLFGANG
Did you think of me?

FABIENNE
Yes... I thought of you...

WOLFGANG
What did you think about me?

> *Silence.*

> What did you think about me?

FABIENNE
That you were dead... That you had died... With a black cloth
on your head... You had died and you were talking... To me...
You were talking to me... You had died and you were talking.
I want to get out. I wish you would die. But you didn't really
die... I just thought it... I wish you would die...because then I
could really think...think of something other than you because
all I ever do is think of you, how I can get away from you
because you have thrown a black cloth over me and I can't see
anything, and all I want is for someone to come and save me,
a hand from the sky, the trees in the garden, the walls to grow
hands and save me.

> *Silence.*

WOLFGANG
Put your clothes on. We'll go out in the car.

29

WOLFGANG and FABIENNE.

WOLFGANG
Sit down. At my feet.

Silence.

Your head here... In my lap.

Silence.

Do you like me stroking your head? What do you feel?

FABIENNE
My head hurts...

WOLFGANG
Again? You have your home, you have me... What else do you want?

FABIENNE
I don't want anything... My head hurts...

Silence.

Tell me what's happening in the world...

WOLFGANG
The world is dying.

FABIENNE
Still?

WOLFGANG
It's slowly giving up the ghost.

Silence.

FABIENNE
How is the world dying? Show me something...

WOLFGANG
Everyone is sick... They cough up blood...

FABIENNE
I cough... Am I going to die?

WOLFGANG
You have me... You are lucky.

FABIENNE
How else are people dying?

WOLFGANG
They are the death of each other.

FABIENNE
Our next-door neighbours? Are they dying?

WOLFGANG
Soon. Their turn will come.

Silence.

FABIENNE
Tell me more things about people... Show me...

WOLFGANG
Yesterday morning...someone fell in the middle of the road...

FABIENNE
In which road?

WOLFGANG
Here...a bit further down from our house...

FABIENNE
How did he fall? Did he slip?

WOLFGANG
He was dizzy... He was dizzy and he fell...

FABIENNE
I get dizzy... Will I fall?

WOLFGANG
You have me.

FABIENNE
And what happened when he fell? Did he die?

WOLFGANG
Not immediately... People gathered...

FABIENNE
What people?

WOLFGANG
Passersby...

FABIENNE
What did they want?

WOLFGANG
They were looking at him.

FABIENNE
Just looking?

WOLFGANG
At first.

FABIENNE
And then?

WOLFGANG
And then they took his watch and his money...

FABIENNE
What else did they take? Show me.

WOLFGANG
Jacket, trousers, shirt, tie...

FABIENNE
Shoes?

WOLFGANG
Yes... Shoes too...

FABIENNE
Underwear?

WOLFGANG
Yes... Underwear too... He ended up naked.

FABIENNE
And did he die?

WOLFGANG
Not yet... Others gathered.

FABIENNE
What did they want?

WOLFGANG
Each one something different...

FABIENNE
What kind of different?

WOLFGANG
Spleen, heart, liver, kidneys, stomach... Each one something different.

FABIENNE
They took them?

WOLFGANG
Yes...everything... There was nothing left.

FABIENNE
And then?

WOLFGANG
Then the road was cleaned up...and the people dispersed.

Silence.

Did you see it?

FABIENNE
Yes... I saw it.

30

WOLFGANG and FABIENNE. WOLFGANG is planting.

FABIENNE
How old am I?

WOLFGANG
Twenty.

FABIENNE
An old woman of twenty.

WOLFGANG
You're not an old woman...

FABIENNE
I don't mind... Better an old woman of twenty than a twenty-year-old knifed in a ditch...

Silence.

What was that girl's name?

WOLFGANG
I don't remember...

FABIENNE
Was she from our city?

WOLFGANG
Not from our city... Somewhere on the border.

FABIENNE
But the war is over...

WOLFGANG
There doesn't need to be a war for people to be stabbed...

FABIENNE
Did they want to rob her?

WOLFGANG
I don't know what they wanted... They stabbed her.

FABIENNE
Where?

WOLFGANG
I told you...at the border...

FABIENNE
In the heart?

WOLFGANG
You don't need to know...

FABIENNE
In the stomach?

WOLFGANG
Don't you be afraid...

FABIENNE
I want you to tell me where...

WOLFGANG
You are in no danger.

FABIENNE
In the throat... They cut her throat... I saw her in my sleep...
She was very sad... She was crying... She was holding her
head and crying...

　　Silence.

　　Wolfgang... I'm going to go...

WOLFGANG
Fine... Get up and go for a walk...

FABIENNE
Not for a walk...

WOLFGANG
Are you sleepy?

FABIENNE
I'm going to leave here...

WOLFGANG
Where do you want to go?

FABIENNE
Out...

WOLFGANG
You can go out if you want...

FABIENNE
Yes...that's what I want...

Silence.

WOLFGANG
You can't do without me... You'll get lost.

FABIENNE
It doesn't matter... They'll find me...

WOLFGANG
In some ditch... You want me to open the hatch again?

FABIENNE
I'm not afraid of it...

WOLFGANG
You'll be afraid if I throw you into the dark...

FABIENNE
I'm not afraid of it... I'm used to it...

WOLFGANG
You can't leave...

Silence.

If you leave, I'll kill myself. You don't want me to kill myself...

Silence.

FABIENNE
A friend of yours came by...

WOLFGANG
A friend of mine? When?

FABIENNE
That's what he told me...a friend of yours.

WOLFGANG
I don't have any friends. When did he come by?

FABIENNE
I know you don't... That's what he told me.

WOLFGANG
Why didn't you call me?

FABIENNE
You were in the toilet...

WOLFGANG
You should have called me.

FABIENNE
It wouldn't have been polite...

WOLFGANG
Next time call me... Don't ever open the door again on your own... Only I open the door.

FABIENNE
I saw him from the window... He didn't seem dangerous...

WOLFGANG
You don't know...

FABIENNE
He insisted... He wanted to give you something...

WOLFGANG
To give me what?

FABIENNE
Something about the car's steering wheel... A leather cover... He remembered that you had been looking for one years ago... He found it and he brought it for you... As a gift.

WOLFGANG
And why did he leave? Why didn't he wait?

FABIENNE
He was in a hurry, he said... He left it and went...

Silence.

I asked him about the war...

WOLFGANG
The war is over...

FABIENNE
I know... I asked him about the effects of the war... About the consequences... He looked at me as if I was an idiot... Not even the old men, he said, remember the war... What consequences?...

WOLFGANG
That was a different war and this a different one...

FABIENNE
I know... That's what I told him...

Silence.

He asked about me... Who I was... If I was your cleaning lady... He said that's what you'd told him... That you had a woman who cleans your house.

WOLFGANG
He passed by one day and saw you in the garden...

FABIENNE
I said no... I am not the woman who cleans the house...

WOLFGANG
What did you say?

FABIENNE
I told him... I am Fabienne. The girl who was lost years ago, in this neighbourhood, I lived in this neighbourhood, you must remember me, I am Fabienne and I'm alive... I've come back. Go and tell my parents... Your friend left at a run...

Silence.

Soon the whole town will know... Everybody...
They'll come and get me.

Silence.

WOLFGANG
You're lying...

FABIENNE
I'm not lying... They'll come and get me...

WOLFGANG
When?

FABIENNE
Soon...

WOLFGANG
When did my friend come...

FABIENNE
When you were in the toilet.

WOLFGANG
You're lying...

FABIENNE
I am not lying... He left at a run... They'll come...

Silence.

WOLFGANG
You were joking... That's what you'll say if they come...
That you were joking... You'll apologise...

FABIENNE
Why should I apologise...

WOLFGANG
I'll apologise... I'll speak to them... You go and hide...

FABIENNE
I am not going to hide...

WOLFGANG
I will speak to them... I'll say that the woman who cleans my house...her name's Fabienne and she remembered the story of the girl...

FABIENNE
I am the girl...

WOLFGANG
It's not who you think.... Go and hide and don't be afraid... They won't find you...

FABIENNE
I'm not afraid...

WOLFGANG
Then don't hide... Put on your glasses and your hat...get in the car...

FABIENNE
I'm not getting in the car again...

WOLFGANG
We're going shopping... We'll say we're about to go shopping... Who is this Fabienne?... We don't know her...

FABIENNE
I am Fabienne...

WOLFGANG
You are my wife...we are going shopping...

FABIENNE
I am Fabienne......

WOLFGANG
Fabienne was lost years ago...

FABIENNE
I am Fabienne...

WOLFGANG
She died...

FABIENNE
I am alive and I've come back.

WOLFGANG
You can't leave... I've got you.

FABIENNE
They're coming...

WOLFGANG
You're mine...

FABIENNE
It's over...

WOLFGANG
Not theirs...

FABIENNE
It's over, Wolfgang...

WOLFGANG
You can't go... I made you... You are a part of me... You are inside me... You can't go... Not now... You see me and I see you... I will always have my eyes on you.

31

WOLFGANG and THE FATHER'S GHOST.

GHOST
Get the keys.

WOLFGANG
Where do you want me to go?

GHOST
Get the keys.

WOLFGANG
And go where?

GHOST
Get into the car and lock the doors.

WOLFGANG
I'm staying here.

GHOST
They're coming with weapons. You haven't got any. You haven't got anything.

WOLFGANG
I haven't got anything.

GHOST
You have me. Get the keys.

WOLFGANG
I'm staying here.

GHOST
Shall I die once more?

WOLFGANG
I've got nothing left now.

GHOST
Don't listen to them...their poisonous voices... You have me... I'll hold you tight.

WOLFGANG
I'm falling, Wolfgang... I'm falling...

GHOST
Get the keys, I'll hold you tight...get in the car and lock the doors.

WOLFGANG
Shall I die once more?

GHOST
They're coming with their weapons to surround you. You have no weapons, you have nothing.

WOLFGANG
I'll stay here and be surrounded. Even if I have got nothing.

GHOST
I'm burning up, Wolfgang... I'm burning up... You let your mother live and I'm burning up. You brought her and shoved her back in my house...so she can ruin us again.

WOLFGANG
A girl...

GHOST
A mouse with wings...you softened for a mouse with wings.

WOLFGANG
The wolves came in sheep's clothing...

GHOST
Their poisonous voices tricked you...

WOLFGANG
They tricked me... What shall I do... Tell me...

GHOST
Come and burn up with me.

WOLFGANG
Burn up...

GHOST
With me... Get the keys. Get into the car and lock the doors.

32

FABIENNE.

FABIENNE
If only I could sit here forever... In the sun.

> *Silence.*

> Nothing's stirring here...

> *Silence.*

When I left and saw all those people around me, the first thing that crossed my mind was to go back, to creep inside my nest again, even deeper inside...

Silence.

Nice hedges... I am envious...

Silence.

When I was little I used to hide behind those hedges... I used to watch you working in the garden... You were engrossed. I liked watching you... But I was also afraid of you... I didn't know why then.

Silence.

I could have killed you... I had the opportunity... The evening when you fell asleep next to me... You were vulnerable...and the garden shears lying there forgotten... I could have snipped off your head.

Silence.

I hold no grudges. You protected me in difficult times... I escaped all sorts of dangers.

Yannis Mavritsakis was born in Montreal in 1964 and has lived in Athens since 1970. He studied acting at the Drama School of the National Theatre in Athens. He graduated in 1986 and worked as an actor until 2003. Since then he has focused on writing. His plays include: *Blind Spot* (2006), *Wolfgang* (2007), *Fucking Job* (2008), *Vitriol* (2010), *Redshift* (2012), *The Invocation of Enchantment* (2014) and *Quasar* (2015).

His plays have been performed at the National Theatre in Athens, the Athens Festival, and other international festivals. *Vitriol* was performed at Festival d'Avignon (summer 2014), under the direction of Olivier Py.

Wolfgang won the prizes Georgios Hortatsis (best play 2008-2010) and Palmares 2010 (Commission Nationale de l'Aide a la creation de textes dramatiques, Paris). It was first performed at the National Theatre (Athens, 2008). It was also performed at the Théâtre de l'Atalante (Paris, 2014-2015) and the Cyprus Theatre Organisation (Nicosia, 2016).

… AND JULIET
by Akis Dimou

Translated by Elizabeth Sakellaridou

... and Juliet

And if love is love lost
How can we find love?

Antonio Porchia, *Voces*

… and Juliet by Akis Dimou
Love as Possibility

Through the course of time Shakespeare's Juliet has grown into the ultimate symbol of surrender to young, unconditional enthusiastic love; to first love – the love one experiences to the full, at the risk of even losing oneself. Her story is that of a romantic love that glorifies the purest feelings in their birth. Juliet dies young and beautiful, her love remaining immaculate and the image of her beloved intact. However, the sacrifice of the young girl in love appears to be an easy way out if compared to the strength required to "stay" in love. Akis Dimou's Juliet stands face to face with the Shakespearean heroine: she is an inverted image of her, bursting with life. She is a woman of indeterminable age, a Juliet ravaged by time, alone in her house – the interior of an old house on a summer night – according to the stage directions. A relic of a glorious past, she addresses some invisible visitors. She speaks her truth with no fear, no need for pretence, and without trying to preserve any myths at all. This woman has dared to live: she has fought, she has been conquered, she has perished for love. She still stands upright, though worn out, and bears proudly the marks of her arrow wounds. The scars on her body and soul are worthy of a brave warrior, because, as she herself exclaims, "Only the brave ones fall in love – remember this." Thus, she dares to live after love is gone, and, most importantly, she dares to speak about it. Only when you have experienced love free from all fear can you speak about it so openly. After the absolute of love, all things leave you indifferent and unmoved. If you have been through a dyadic existence you cannot return to your former condition.

This monologue, deeply related to poetry, constitutes a tortured truth, balancing between dream and fantasy. Its innate musicality and linguistic rhythm flow smoothly, thus producing an unprecedented outburst of emotions, while the whisper of death overshadows everything. The heroine could be as much a man as a woman. She could be herself or not. Her story might as well be her own as someone else's, which she once heard and is now recounting. Dimou's play is a hymn to conqueror-love but also to any human who dares to dive in its fierce waters and then swim back to the shore in the knowledge that s/he won't be the same person any longer. Whatever the case, Juliet is a free individual, an anti-hero who sheds all symbolism, who liberates herself through her open confession and achieves catharsis.

Despite the fact that this text is Dimou's first play (written in 1994), it already reveals the author's theatrical genius and bears all the basic traits of his dramaturgy. Dimou is a major name in the domain of contemporary Greek theatre. He has a distinct style of his own which does not try to romanticise or imitate reality, but to reconstruct it through his sharp poetic vision without any romantic embellishment. He explores the secret landscapes of love and charts the darkest paths of human (especially female) psychology. At the same time his plays are in a continuous dialogue with other great texts and writers. As a dramatist, Dimou uses bold and vivid language, whose poetic style is counterbalanced by his underground, sarcastic humour. His works do not seek a social background but find their roots in the human soul. This is why they have an immediate, affective appeal to the audience. ... and Juliet is a response to all love, "because love, my dear Sir, is just a possibility."

Irini Mountraki, Theatrologist/Theatre Critic
Head of International Relations of the National Theatre of Greece
Founder of Greek Play Project (www.greek-theatre.gr)

A woman. Interior of an old house. A summer night.

I won't get up, please forgive me.

I have forgotten how to receive people: the movements you make, the words you say on such occasions. Visits have lost all interest for me. They simply remind me that I am alone for one more night.

I expect nothing from others. It's their own illusion if they still expect something from me. Please, don't take this personally. This is the only way I can address you: as if I am alone. As if you are not here. Or as if you are – which of course is the same to me. *(Pause.)* Do you find me rude? Difficult? Eccentric? Oh, I don't care, I assure you, I don't care at all. I have no more pride that could be hurt by your criticism, I have no face to protect from the echo of a bad impression. Such concerns belong to women of the world. Women with husbands, children and relatives, friends, admirers – or lovers, why not? Women who have been awarded the splendor of mediocrity, the medals of order and domesticity, ones who mistook the cheap lifestyle for real royalty, for whom their court's morose flatteries become the salt of their redundant existence. But for a woman whose life is contrary to all this, what could be the meaning of a stranger's flattery?

Therefore, shield yourself against my disdain and do not make a judgment. Keep your conclusions to yourself. If not, you will only cause me amusement, but you won't see me laugh.

It's been a long time since I have unlearned how to laugh.

Isn't it unusually hot tonight? As if the air is thinning, melting. And this indefinable fragrance in the air... If you have brought me flowers, then please, leave them somewhere by your side. And take them back with you on your way out. You obviously know nothing about me if you came all this way out here to bring me a bunch of fresh cyclamens. I mean...any polite gesture repels me, any charming appeal leaves me as indifferent as the change of seasons in the outer world. A stretched arm offering me a bunch of flowers mocks my eternal mourning. Unless it is only a bouquet of young shoots, like the ones destined for sepulchral decoration. Unless you are offering it in modesty, as a suitable tribute to my darling tomb. If this is the case, you can place it where you think most appropriate. And leave it there to rot.

The mountains start here: beyond the collection of wines which are cooling in the cellar. There are times when I feel – steeped as I am in drink – that my feet can't hold me on my way down the steps and then back up here with a fresh bottle under my arm.

I am addicted to drinking. I began with just a little at first, then as time went by I started filling the glass more frequently. I love wine: its colour, its smell, the images on the glass which meet my eyes – these eyes which were so much absorbed by one single image in the past. Getting drunk becomes harder and harder for me but I can still fool myself. I hear distant voices, horses galloping. I see roads folding into other roads. I hear footsteps travelling out here. They tread through the woods, they walk across the cedars and the ebony trees, making their way through the prickly bushes, they stop at the gate, in silence. The only noise heard is the cracking of stones under their boots. For just a moment I feel as if my life is changing, as if I am springing up into the air, invigorated. I make new friends. A temptation curls at my door, waiting for me to yield. *(Pause.)* But nothing happens… Silence.

The house retreats to its foundations, as if defeated. It had so longed to flee. *(Short pause.)*

Can't you see it? Making chaos is easy. One single brush stroke on the canvas still holds the walls together, the doors are eliminated, the roof is ripped open. *(Pause.)* My last remaining possessions have become invisible. Our embraces have gnawed them away.

Since that moment nothing can protect me any longer.

My feet are cold. I shall put on my slippers – do you mind? But first I must remember where I left them, and where I must place my steps in order to come back here. I have forgotten how to move about in the house. Except for this cosy corner, the rest of it looks alien, as if inhabited by strangers while I stand by and watch their movements in silence. *(Pause.)*

Sometimes I have a strong desire to roam about in the rooms as before.

I must make haste before night falls, at the precise moment when the light is fading on my verandah. It is the most beautiful time of day.

I want to feel again the furniture warm up at my approach, to hear again the swish of a curtain, to feel the floor cracking with pleasure, to hear the delicate music of a glass fruit bowl, or the murmur of the kettle in the kitchen – just as in the old days. I could loiter in the house for hours but I didn't mind. Every tour was an adventure, a journey full of startling events. I never knew what was hidden behind things and where, even though I had wandered through all of the rooms time and again. Ignorance was once the girls' privilege. *(Pause.)* Oh how dear that house was to me, how wildly do I miss its company, the shadows on the windows, the flickering reflections of the lamp on the ceiling. *(Pause.)*

"O I have bought the mansion of a love,

But not possess'd it, and though I am sold,

Not yet enjoy'd." *(Pause.)*

Occasionally I tell myself: you must get up at last. You must go back to see and smell. But I feel heavy, incapable of the slightest movement. I therefore stay here, within these few square meters, which are still under my control. And I project all things here, I transfer them here. I imagine I am going up and down the stairs, I invent new games under the corridor arches, my armchair becomes ten different chairs, nine people attend on me reverently, they rise and wait for me to sit, and dinner starts – that dinner which had been interrupted so many years ago... *(Pause.)* I rest my head on the back of my armchair and start to dream. A small tree pushes up through the floor mosaic. I embrace it. I kiss it deep in the mouth. My lips burn from the taste of its sap. I take a needle and thread to sew a fence around it, then stitch a thousand birds among its branches. Every morning I wake up shuddering slightly under its shade, just as in the presence of my old love.

Please, come closer, here, over my shoulder... Look carefully. Can you see the orchards? They are barren, their soil is dry, yellow like the saliva of insects. Can you discern at the far end the rain in hiding? Like a motionless old hag, turned to stone. The cracking of lightning has not been heard for years...

Oh, don't stand like this. Move away from that spot. You never know when God will strike. *(Pause.)*

There used to be a chestnut tree over there. A beautiful tree, full of life: that was my consolation. Every time he left, I would rush to hide in its branches. It prolonged its shadow for me to sit under it. Its leaves cheered me up. They wouldn't permit the beams of any other sun except his eyes to fall upon me. Migrant birds would come and look at me in the eyes trustily. I thought their chirp would last for years. I dug up the soil with my fingers, reached the deep fresh roots of the tree and talked to them. I kept all the words locked up in my mouth every time he took me in his arms. I whispered them to the tree and when we met again I knew he had overheard them. I was never surprised when he brought an answer to a question I had never asked. *(Pause.)* That is what love is: to prevent words. Not to let a word soil your lips, and to make everything sound sweet as if spoken. *(Pause.)* It was with him alone that I forgot all my words: the purple adjectives, the carnivorous verbs, the complying conjunctions, the glaring adverbs. Away from the domination of language, how beautifully my body swirled! How clearly I could hear the babbling flow of my blood. Oh how my breath rocked the world!

I am sure that you speak beautifully. You look intelligent... and educated. I guess people enjoy listening to you. And how beautifully your thought must be stitched to your speech. How appropriately, how gracefully, how eloquently you must defend your life against any malevolent interlocutors, against any dishonest fellow players. Have you ever fallen in love – I wonder. Did you happen to know Romeo? *(Pause.)*

Please turn around so that I can see you. You, too, can look at me. The more I talk to you the more I feel I can trust you. Oh, come now, do not blush. You may smoke if you like. Smoking can be beneficial when you have no other way to mollify a moment of aggression – good or bad, it doesn't matter. *(Short pause.)*

I usually leave the back gate open but nobody comes – perhaps it's because they all know how much I dislike visitors, or perhaps the world doesn't find me interesting any longer. In any case, what benefit could one gain from me? I can only bring back a memory of bloodshed, but who would ever wish to recall anything of the kind? *(Pause.)*

My back yard has looked desolate for so many years now. Untrodden. There is just a tiny, tired stream flowing through it, crimson and thin, like blood trickling down the temple of a man who was killed by his own noble hand: it is the blood that I was talking about just a moment ago...

No, no, he didn't mean any harm. He simply wanted to prove how grave and fatal an accidental handshake could be – or, a fleeting touch in the curve of the palm. Then came the kiss, on the cut of the neck, on the breast or the shoulder... *(Long pause.)*

Have you ever asked yourself exactly what it is that we fall in love with in another person? Have you ever turned this riddle in your mind? What is it about this person that raises the dormant armies of our senses and throws us unarmed into a battle already lost? Where exactly lies the power of the other – the power that pushes us naked into the minefield of a yet unknown embrace? Oh, come, poke into your past and try to remember – if, of course, you can recall such a rare memory. What did that mortal dagger that hit you look like?

Was it liquid like a blue gaze, or solid like a firm step, or ethereal like desirous arms closing in a deep embrace which reaches down to the roots?...

Oh, you are wasting your time. You will never find an answer to this. Whoever has tried to interpret love has never been in love. Only deafening silence can match the absolute nature of such a gift, a silence strewn with the unspeakable particles of the universe that spark for just a second – which is precisely the duration of a gasping embrace.

I can now remember…

Before I saw him, I already knew him well, down to the slightest detail, the knot of his cape, and that small cyclamen on the buckle of his belt – a girlish sign, a hint of tenderness, enough to suggest that his sword was no more than a silly convention which demanded all of the boys of his generation to be warriors – a mask unable to hide a sensitive and nonchalant soul. I admired him in secret. I loved him in silence. I have always depended on him. I turned to him for encouragement so that I could continue to live through my whole body, though under protection, with my voice muffled.

When one afternoon somebody at last introduced him to me on the steps of the square, I could find nothing else to say except "I am in a hurry, my friends hate waiting" – and leaving with my shawl flying loose. It was later that I learned how beautifully he danced in the centre of the fire; with how much skill and rare concentration he would press the daggers to his throat, without causing one drop of blood, without stopping singing for one single moment.

If *he* was not the man for me, then who would ever be? *(Pause.)*

For days afterwards I lived through his dance. I thought of him intensely, insistently. I was totally taken by his eyes. In my mind I devoted myself to him like those believers who worship a saint and carry the holy image in themselves wherever they are, wherever they go, waiting for a revelation, fervently waiting for the miracle to happen.

The thought of him set me on fire, my sleep soaked in water; I lost myself in its depths. I was seduced by my very devotion. I confused my movements, my saliva thinned, my words became wet and slid out before I could utter. I moved about in the house with complete indifference to the gossiping gaze of the servants who wondered about my unmotivated loitering. My hair got tangled in the furniture like the antlers of a deer caught in the thick shrubs. I measured my breath and wondered: so little of it left – how could I possibly still be alive?

Tender winds set me on sail, they rocked me, then, sweeping forcefully across me, they ravaged me.

I brought him close to me, next to me, I held him in me with a blind, masculine force, foreign to my gender.

A fractional thought of him was enough to lift me up – not exactly by elevating me, but elating me, yes, while I actually bumped upon the ground. The nurse would find me lying unconscious on the floor, not breathing. When I recovered, I would fall into a complete reverie. I was alone again but in my bloodstream it felt as if I were two people in a tight embrace. My veins would go numb, my body revitalized by a refreshing fever which would make my legs shiver, as if training them for longer trips to take.

I burst into tears quite spontaneously as I saw the meadows turn green. The fields were so full with harvest, like a heart brimming with happiness. Time was my friend, the hours were on my side, the light of darkness built bridges for me to cross over. I would sit at the window to do my embroidery. I felt like fine mist, like a swallow. I stitched red hearts onto pillowcases. I mended my old tunic, surprised that it was still large enough for me – as if I had never grown into an adult. (Pause.)

The summer was coming. I would go down to spin by the well, the moon got entangled in my spinning wheel, stars would splash in the water and my thread would fill with blossoms. A funereal bliss filled me inside.

And this deeply disturbed me as if foreshadowing a salutary loss, a night of murder. (Pause.)

Since then, he came four more times.

He waited in hiding until he could get me alone.

"Fain would I dwell on form, fain, fain, deny

What I have spoke."

Fear, my good Sir, is a road closed to love. It is a rough path full of snake nests and vile weed. At its far end, out of reach, you can discern the all-green clearing of love. But this is the only way to struggle for your deepest emotion: you have to tread this path, with your feet bleeding on the sharp stones, elbowing through carnivorous, trailing plants, ready to suck upon your skin. You have to look always ahead, to look into yourself, where your burning desire has its seat, where yearning spreads its blue sky, where the heart beats in solitude, where a fire burns in the middle of the ocean.

Falling in love means to move on, to go ahead., to pierce and be pierced, and go far away, in order to reach, at some point, the luminous destiny allotted to you.

It means to arrive: barefoot, soaking in sweat, exhausted, bruised, with broken fingernails, no teeth, burnt eyelids, swollen knees, pierced hands, your voice grating on the syllables of I love you... And yet only then do you arrive.

Because love, my dear Sir, is just a possibility.

It means I can.

It means I know and I do not know simultaneously.

It means I commit a crime and I am also fully innocent.

It means I am paralyzed before the possibility of revelation but I am also empowered, dear Sir, by this fear. *(Pause.)*

Only the brave ones fall in love – remember this. The others simply fool their own dreams. *I* belonged to the former. *(Pause.)*

Therefore, let me do away with society, away with the shouts and the hostility of parents, or with the nurse's advice. Away with menaces and curses, with the razor-sharp glances of my father, the clattering terror emanating from my mother's high heels, the old men shuffling the tarot cards at the cafe and sneering viciously when I passed by, the women weaving death in the seclusion of their homes, the blood I could already hear throbbing in my ears. I lived fully immersed in my desire. Let Verona perish in ruins. I have known no other home except my room's balcony. The only place I recognized as my birthplace was that iron-fenced balcony.

Please come closer. I want to show you something.

Do you see this pack of manuscripts? If you come closer, you will get caught in the thick cobweb of words. The reflection of dark calligraphy will strike your eyes even though the ink is so dry. The writing has so much faded that you will have to try hard – not to read it, surely, I could dream of nothing more impious than this – but to simply discern the traces of an almost invisible handwriting. *(Short pause.)*

Hold the pack in your hands for a few minutes.

These pages are so soft to touch, as fine as a pair of silk socks, ideal for a maiden's fingers, which are so used to the prick of a sewing needle, but also so sensitive to the utterance of an "I adore you" which has poured its desire onto paper. These are the letters I received from him. I had to take a thousand precautions, I had to invent a thousand clever tricks which would have made even the most consummate state schemer feel ashamed for his own naïve, trivial methods.

I have no other possessions except these papers, just these words which he never articulated. If caresses could speak, if a glance knew how to utter, you would find their voice transcribed here. I am lucky that sighs know no grammar – which makes them sound so precious.

Since then, I never read these letters again, but I often take them in my hands and flick through them in ecstasy. I make an extreme effort to slip through the sentences without cutting myself. At other times I permit myself to read, through the corner of my eye, "oh how much do I love you", "oh my joy", "stay" – each syllable generating new tears. *(Pause.)*

I find no meaning in this activity any longer, only a constructive pain reminding me that I am still indebted to daggers, and that the breath of death is approaching. *(Short pause.)*

I never answered those letters. I have always had difficulty with words, I must have been a mis-speller by spite, following an idiosyncratic spelling code which I very much enjoyed at the time that I was writing my diary. But I was afraid it might look strange or ridiculous in the eyes of an unknown reader.

The person who fetched the letters did not have anything to take back in return from me. Just a handful of jasmines, a pair of coral earrings, a small deserted beehive or a tiny red stone – an empowering memento from the monastery of Saint Sebastian, the patron saint of young couples on their new path of life. It was with such humble gifts that I responded to his double-edged words. *(Pause.)*

Now I write to him without taking up either pen or paper. I talk to him through my deepest, my most precious, most crystalline voice, which you would shudder to hear in your dreams. It is the voice that only the dead can hear.

Then the rest of the events took place, which you must have heard of. No one can claim ignorance to these facts. Criers, tavern keepers, servants, coachmen – they all took good care to spread the news. The parson also chattered about it. My own friends did not act any better. *(Pause.)* We resorted to devilish tricks, tried various methods and rehearsed our deaths to make them final. *He* succeeded in the end. *I* failed – being always the lesser partner, the minor one, the less fortunate of the two, the more bound to life – being a woman. *(Pause.)*

Now that I ruminate over the past in a more detached manner, I can say that *this is* how things should have been. Somebody should always remain alive. Even after the end, one person should still stand upright there, in order to meet the horror, to suffer, to bleed and to be torn apart, to feed the blackest lion in the mouth, to despair and never find relief. Somebody must always stay behind, mutilated, disabled, torn to pieces, in order to glorify an inglorious love and – with the cry of defeat fading on her lips – to collapse on the ground like a hollow mass of rust, like a non-sailing mast of a ship, rotting in the sand. (Pause.)

I don't want to talk about those things. I was merely carried away. Night is falling. There is a royal moon tonight. Do you like the moon? I love it so much. If only you knew how to penetrate my thoughts… I keep a secret landscape in my mind – an innocuous part of nature that the passage of time did not burn down. It is full of fresh, fragrant waters, even the veins of stones are in bloom. There is always a heavy, proud moon over there. I often dream of going there. It is a Tuesday, a lonely day like all the rest. I am walking across the gardens. The royal peacocks are picking at the begonias. In the thick foliage little birds are shaking the lingering drops of rain off their wings. They are small and soft, like questioning thoughts that have stayed unanswered. The closer I go, the more the landscape recedes to the background: it is an unapproachable territory unyielding to my steps. I can never reach it. I am back again to the same rough desert.

Do you notice how the shadows change colour at this time of day? (Pause.)

"Come gentle night, come loving black-brow'd night,

Give me my Romeo, and when he shall die,

Take him and cut him out in little stars,

And he will make the face of heaven so fine,

That all the world will be in love with night,

And pay no worship to the garish Sun."

One Sunday afternoon, when I was eight years old, my parents took me out for a walk. Our house was high up and in order to reach the centre of the town we had to cover a fairly long distance. We dressed early – it was hardly afternoon yet – and the coachman made the horses gallop. The clouds were low, their underbelly almost touched the roof of the carriage but this didn't mean rain. It was May, the month of the lark and the weasel. As I was gazing lazily through the window, at the road's turn, my glance was caught by another window, that of a stone house with a thin trailing plant on its brown walls. A woman was kneading. She was a fleshy, middle-aged woman, with a rich bosom and strong arms, bared up to her shoulders. Her hair was done tightly up around her head, running loose only at the back of her neck. Sparks of sweat glittered on her brow and neck. She wiped them off with the back of her hand and went on kneading.

All of a sudden, I saw a man approach her noiselessly from behind so that he took her unawares. He clasped her tight and smacked a kiss at the nape of her neck – a hot, sweaty, rough kiss. The woman started laughing. She turned around and embraced him, her arms sticky with the steaming dough. They must have kissed again and again that day. At that early age, I knew nothing about what I had just witnessed, and my puzzlement was soon drowned in the lemonade I drank at the square. But today, ah, you can't possibly guess how often I long to have been that anonymous woman, that particular woman with her dough, her sweat and her kiss! With her miserable but blessed destiny! *(Pause.)*

I wonder: is such a desire an impiety? Isn't it a blasphemy to be disloyal to the exquisite chaos I was destined to experience?

I leave a crack at every door. There is always a blind left open at the window in order to let in some light in the falling night – when I get oblivious. A dwarfish shadow enters, it curls at my feet, it warms its hands on my legs, I can feel it is trembling. I want to get up, to clap my hands: "Give me some sun" – I turn angrily to the maids who are taking too long to light the lamp. I do nothing. I stand motionless watching the shadow shrink. Its breath is heavy, its last word is bitter, like a letter announcing the end of something. Before dawn, it has consumed itself, giving out a slow, magnificent, scented flame. *(Pause.)*

This is myself.

Distant.

Sorrowful.

Diminished.

I am the dust that has covered the balcony.

I am the snail that has fallen asleep in the flower pot.

My most ragged stockings.

My golden sandals that have been torn.

The withered mint; the dried up mastic.

The dirty marble stone on the front porch.

The hard seed of lavender which has failed to shoot.

The knocker on the door: a small rusty fist.

I am the smell the boys give out when they dream of seduction.

Because *I* was seduced first. *(Pause.)*

There is no story for me any longer.

Please don't look at me like this. I know I am growing old. I have told time that I am at its mercy. It can ravage me, it can crush me. I do not expect any reward for my former kindness. *(Pause.)*

There are moments when I do not think of him at all and this is a glorious victory, I can hardly restrain my cries of triumph.

The traces of memory can be uprooted even if they are deep. Exile is wise, wise and generous as no homeland ever can be. *(Pause.)*

I have always been like this, an adolescent girl in happiness, an old woman in sorrow. Age is contingent, insignificant. Nothing can wound me any longer. My own breath exists simply because I have willfully turned myself into a common person.

Nor do I bear any grievance against that summer which we
lived together. I can therefore recall him without the fear of
drowning or of sinking in the seaweed. I can become tender
again. Forgiveness spreads on my cheeks – it's OK that I
haven't lived my life, it's absolutely fine.

It is enough for me to see from my window, far away,
the mountains resting quietly, like lovers hugging together
in their shared sleep, when bodies go dry and lips are numb
and hardly moving. *(Pause.)*

I imagine... I am out for a walk... I walk up the hill, the hunters
greet me, taking off their caps... I stoop and take food from
their palms, I let myself be seduced, feigning ignorance.
The fresh grass caresses my hooves, there are no prickly shrubs
anywhere around and all traps are innocent. In the distance
I can discern the stone chimney of my house attracting all of
the light for itself. I give a deep muffled sob – which sounds
so much like my laugh – writhing in pain on the ground, my
entrails all poured out, their gun points smoking. *(Pause.)*

At some other moments I imagine that I can lift the darkness in
one hand, I hold it lightly and then I turn it three times round
my neck, like the string of pearls I used to wear at the age
of fifteen, or like a noose. *(Pause.)* I go for a minute out onto
the landing to reminisce: of wounded passions, of laughs of
yonder, of drops of poison that permanently stained my bridal
dress, most of all to remember a love that was consumed in
words.

I always ask questions in silence, without expecting an answer.
It is totally in vain to try to unlock the abyss. My eyes fill with
tears despite myself. Ah, pity for our wasted youth. But I can't
bear any more sorrow. Whatever sprouts inside us is only
destined to wither...like the crocuses, or the anemones.
That's the law of nature, of life, isn't it?

In the end blood is always engulfed by fire, until the sea
congeals in our hands and our salty kisses taste like poison.
(Pause.)

I stay out on the landing till late.

A horse passes by.

Romeo is holding fast to its neck as the horse gallops on, pulling along a crimson sky with its hooves.

"Hello," I shout, and then "Happy death." *(Pause.)*

I shudder at the thought of the events to come, the minor ones.

"Decency," is what my noble descent demands, "keep your head up, your sorrow up, up"... Sobbing always comes at a precise moment, it lasts for a little while. Then I go back into the house. *(Long pause.)*

I am shipwrecked. And I am rotting away, on a seabed which you call "the world". But I still delude myself with perfumes, I paint my toenails violet, I replace the worn fringe of my shawl, I mend my gloves... I spend my nights in secret – away from mirrors.

And every morning I wash my eyelids with rosewater. One should know how to preserve dreams in life, also how to make nightmares harmless. *(Pause.)*

I visualise the future as a dark cave. I am already in it. Do not take this as an exaggeration. Look at my hands: they are torn by the rocks and the gush of the waves.

I've had enough of the sea. My voyage is over.

Let others be sweetened by love. I have been bent in two. And still I can't fit in.

I have caused you sorrow, I can see it. Oh, please, do not feel sad. At least not for me. There is so much love around you and in you that the slightest sympathy for my desolate state is a meaningless waste. Hold back your tears. You may need them sooner or later. Then you may think of me for a while, and sob in solitude afterwards, not for my loneliness but for your own precious affliction. *(Pause.)*

On a starlit night, I would go to the lake in the coach, or ride the motorcycle of the caretaker's son. You probably met him on your way here. He is a beautiful, somewhat misty boy – full of hands. I would very much like to bury my feet in the sand and stand there for hours, watching the oarsmen sweat in rowing. Have you ever watched rowing at night? You would be enchanted by the movement of the oars, their strict symmetry as they cut the water, opening silver holes on the quiet surface of the lake.

I would return before dawn. I would shake the sand off my feet. The floor was strewn with its fair dust. I didn't make haste to clean it away. I would leave it there to creak lightly every time I stepped on it barefoot. I would let it remind me of that evening…at the lake…when I, with my full name, all my name in that other name, at that dazzling moment, with all my eyes, all my hands, all my heart swallowing me; all my life in that one evening, before death…before I…my own half… oh my darling…less than my half…before being left alone and then nothing…nobody…no soul anywhere…nobody in me anywhere…until I too become absent from my own body…

Please, do not come back here. The presence of strangers upsets me. Whenever I speak, it is as if I dig into my own body, as if I go down into my own flesh, and when I return to the world around me I feel empty, devastated and unarmed, all the parts of my body have been destroyed, my senses shattered. I have no face.

I can only ask you to forget me. *(Pause.)*

Please, go away. Do you not pity me?

The colours fade away. A wind will rise to drive away the days of my sorrow.

It will adorn my breath with spearmint leaves.

An eternal night will come, a personal night, all mine, which won't be disrupted by rough afternoons and disturbing sunsets.

Absence will no more grate on me.

I will be a kind old woman, some other woman will enjoy my memories. I'll have made friends with your shadow, I will not quarrel with it for withholding your body from me.

You will live with me here just as we had dreamt of doing so many times in the past. We will be completely cured from that death.

You will sit here by my side. You will lie down at my feet, like a small bird, a token from our long-dead youth.

You will sing to me like a human, telling me ethereal lies, incredible truths. You will promise me seductive embraces.

You will unbutton your feathers in order to feel lighter, you will switch off the lights with your beak so that nobody can see us: we are not made for the world of humans.

Afterwards, you will perch on my bed.

I will bring you water, hot coffee, bread crumbs.

Wiping off the ashes from my eyes, I will look at you laughing. I will embrace you and the darkness of time will recede in fright.

Somebody must water the statues tonight.

It is so blazing hot out there…and – I can feel it – it will be too long before the rain returns.

July 1994 - November 1995

Note: The three passages in quotation marks have been taken from Shakespeare's *Romeo and Juliet*.

Akis Dimou was born in Greece. He studied Law at Aristotle University of Thessaloniki, where he also did an MA in Penal Code and Criminology. His first theatre work, produced in 1995, was the monologue ... *and Juliet*. Since then, twenty-four of his plays have been performed in various subsidised and private theatres in Greece. His plays have also been translated into English, French, Spanish and Portuguese and have been staged in Britain, Belgium, Spain and Portugal.

Akis Dimou lives in Thessaloniki.

HUNGRY
by Charalampos Giannou

Translated by Charalampos Giannou

The Dysfunctional Family:
Deprivation and the Need for Fulfilment

Charalambos Giannou, a writer of Greek-Cypriot origin, made his first appearance on the Greek stage in 2008 with his play *Falling Down the Stairs*. He has since written another seven plays, which have been staged in Greece, Cyprus and Spain and have received various awards. His distinct dramatic style, which avoids the traps of topicality and is mainly based on a sparse, almost elliptical but also dense dialogue, has already drawn the attention of both audience and critics, placing him amongst the most promising new Greek playwrights.

His play *Hungry*, which focuses on the dysfunctional family and the psychic disturbances it can lead to, received the Greek State Award for Best Play in 2014. Its storyline, boldly extreme and stripped of all spatiotemporal specificity, refers to intense dramatic situations that can happen at any place and time. What is more, the grotesque treatment of the material and the nearly mechanistic action, deprived of any emotional depth, as well as its tragicomic character – all tend to undermine the realism of the play and link it with the distant echo of the European theatre tradition of the absurd. The sense of the absurd is further enhanced through the use of elements of abstraction, mainly to be found in the language of the text. The parallel use of classical dramatic elements, such as plot structure (beginning, climax, conclusion), the fast pace of action (rising plot and suspense) and the Aristotelian unity of time-place-action give the text an exciting theatricality.

Six characters are involved in the plot of the play: the mother, the father, the son, the doctor, the grandmother and the uncle. The son, who is emotionally frozen, refuses to communicate with his external environment and his parents resort to medical assistance. While the doctor is trying to find some code of communication, the parents exhaust themselves in a struggle of mutual extermination, blaming each other for the son's psychic collapse. Incapable of understanding his basic needs for food, security and of course cuddling and love, they feel humiliated for their failure in their parental roles. Burdened with such negative feelings, they attempt to deal with him for the first time in their lives.

In the course of this endeavour, what also comes to the surface is their own psychic deficiency. A sense of "crisis" is clearly felt right from the beginning but reaches its climax only gradually. The mother attacks the father with a knife and kills the doctor instead. The doctor lies half-dead and is finished off by the father. Then it is the grandmother's turn to become the lever of action. Her apparently innocent arrival to the house pushes the action forwards and actually generates terrible consequences within the play. A violent gesture on the part of the mother against the grandmother will cause the latter's death. A succession of mistakes and clownish situations lead to the end, where the cycle of suppressed anger will close once again with violence. The unravelling of all the scenes now looks like the natural outcome of the surrounding morbid atmosphere that the author has skilfully created.

The characters are in a raving state, at the uncertain borderline between external and internal reality. Mechanisms are activated which had been slumbering for a long time. The son, who had assumed a totally passive attitude so far, now attempts to take up an active role as an act of resistance to his supposed extinction by the others. The ending oscillates between fantasy and reality. Where there is an absolute absence of love and decency; where there is no possibility for a healthy emotional discharge, surrealism takes over.

This is not the first time that Giannou deals with family dysfunctionality. This theme has become a motif in his dramaturgy. He had tackled it before in some other plays of his, such as *Falling Down the Stairs* (2008), *a doghouse* (2011), *Her Life as Dead* (2011) and *Home* (2014).

In *Hungry* the writer asks some fundamental questions. Centring on the nuclear family, which forms the vital cell of the biological and social texture, he examines to what degree the behaviour of the individual can be understood within the frame of this primary social group and how far personality and psychic disturbances can be explained in this context. In Giannou's theatre psychological problems are redefined as symptoms of the system of relationships and their dynamics, as developed among family members who share a life together.

The myth of the play brings forward two extreme cases of the dysfunctional family: at one end lies the cold and distanciating familial environment which destroys the individual and renders it completely passive or extremely aggressive (mother-father-son). At the other end lies the equally harmful, overprotective situation, which stifles the autonomy and the creative development of the child, rendering it emotionally dependent and incapable of forming a healthy personality (grandmother and uncle).

Obviously, it is not accidental that the characters have no names but are only defined by their position in the family. Giannou is looking for the original cause of psychic disturbance and tackles the problem at its root. What he is interested in is the psychopathology of the hermetic family form. The corrosive influence of the wider sociohistorical environment does not concern him; this is why spatiotemporal references are absent from his text.

The action unravels in the rooms of a house which could be placed anywhere. These rooms constitute the only scenic environment of the play, thus enhancing a claustrophobic effect. Historical time remains undefined while dramatic and scenic time collapse into one. This conflation of time helps precipitate action and intensifies the spectators' expectations for a final solution.

It must be noted, however, that the most distinctive feature of Giannou's theatre is his special use of language. It is sparse, rid of all superfluous elements, in the form of fast repartee, which keeps tight the dramatic economy of the play. The dialogue follows the codes of orality, preserving the naturalness of communication through overlapping, interruption, correction, hesitation, fragmentation. At the same time the author inscribes in the characters' speeches all the necessary information concerning the construction of dramatic situations and the portrayal of characters and their conflicts.

This is in fact a language where the desire for love simmers under all stage action throughout the play but it actually forbids discussion about love. There are no monologues in the play that could explicate the characters' motives. Giannou's interest seems to focus on the "here and now" of stage action only to reveal the hidden aspect of things, the repressed desires of the characters. It thus manages to represent what lies between the lines.

Finally, the pivotal image of the play is the condition of hunger, which can even lead to death. The son suffers from biological hunger because – according to the dramatic myth – his mother has completely forgotten to provide him with food for over a week – at least this is what *she* conceptualises retrospectively. But the great handicap that all the characters suffer from is their inability to realise their *emotional* "hunger." This is the core of their tragic dimension. The notion of hunger, therefore, develops into a symbol of lack; of psychic deprivation; of a craving for fulfilment; and also of a futile search for the meaning of existence that only love can appease.

Constantina Ziropoulou
Dr. of Theatre Studies
Lecturer at the Hellenic Open University

Characters

FATHER

MOTHER

SON

DOCTOR*

GRANDMOTHER*

UNCLE*

*the last three are played by the same actor

The parents' room.

FATHER
We might as well accept it.
Our son is a psychopath.

MOTHER
(Whispering.) Shhh.

FATHER
Once and for all, a psychopath.

MOTHER
(Whispering.) Shhh.

FATHER
Don't tell me to shhh. You know I'm right.

MOTHER
(Whispering.) The doctor...

FATHER
The doctor what? He is the only one who hasn't noticed yet.

MOTHER
(Whispering.) Stop it. Do you want him to hear you?

FATHER
(Whispering.) If only he would – maybe then he'd clear out of here.

MOTHER
... So that's it? You're giving up on him now?

FATHER
Is that what you think I meant?

MOTHER
Forget it! He is doing much better now/

FATHER
Why? Has he opened his mouth? Has he said anything without my knowledge?

MOTHER
It's still too early.

FATHER
Or too late!

MOTHER
What's your problem?! Just tell me that!

FATHER
What's yours?

MOTHER
Don't you know?

FATHER
So it's my fault again!

MOTHER
I didn't say it was your fault.

FATHER
Fine, spit it out then and let's get it over with.

MOTHER
(She shakes her head.) Let it go – You don't understand me.

FATHER
What about me? Who understands me?

Pause.

FATHER
How did this happen to us?

MOTHER
Let it go – don't go there now.

FATHER
I can't get my head around it.

MOTHER
We've been through this/

FATHER
A little while ago he was happy as can be.

MOTHER
He wasn't happy as can be – and it wasn't "a little while ago".

FATHER
What have we ever done to him?

MOTHER
Just let it go.

FATHER
It's our fault…

MOTHER
Oh, for goodness sake.

FATHER
Isn't that right?

MOTHER
I agree it didn't happen on its own.

FATHER
Right, we woke up one morning and said let's turn our child into a psychopath. As if we didn't have anything better to do.

MOTHER
(Whispering.) He isn't a psychopath.

FATHER
A psychopath, once and for all.

MOTHER
(To herself.) I should have kept my mouth shut.

FATHER
Perhaps even worse than that.

MOTHER
You do realize you're driving yourself mad, don't you?

FATHER
I'm not the mad one here. *(He lowers his voice.)* And for your information, there's no history of psychopaths on my side of the family.

MOTHER
Oh, right, now it's my family that's at fault.

FATHER
Not all your family, just/

MOTHER
Leave my mother out of it.

FATHER
Why?

MOTHER
Because I've had it up to here – do you understand?

FATHER
Isn't she the one who made him what he is?

MOTHER
Of course, it's everyone's fault except yours.

FATHER
Isn't she the one who spoiled him?

MOTHER
It's what grandmothers do; they spoil their grandchildren.

FATHER
That's what she did to your brother, isn't it?

MOTHER
I was wondering when you'd bring that up...

FATHER
That woman has destroyed generation upon generation...

MOTHER
Don't make me start on your mother.

FATHER
A thousand times better than yours.

MOTHER
Take it back. If you had the tiniest bit of shame/

FATHER
Yes, my mother might be a bad person/

MOTHER
Might be?!

FATHER
She did one good thing in her life, you know.

MOTHER
What? Have you?

FATHER
She left me to my own devices.

MOTHER
And what good did that do you?

FATHER
I made my own way. I became who I am.

MOTHER
And are you satisfied with the result?

FATHER
I do the best I can.

MOTHER
Believe me, you can do better.

FATHER
You can say whatever you like; I feel I've been very lucky.

MOTHER
Lucky? When you weren't even loved by your own mother.

FATHER
Too much love makes a person a good-for-nothing.

MOTHER
And what does 'no love' do?

> *Pause.*

FATHER
Well, yours was a close call too, wasn't it?

MOTHER
Please don't start on my brother now.

FATHER
Why not? He's my hero... He sits in his room all day and waits for your mother to feed and clothe him and...

MOTHER
You have no right

FATHER
Does she wipe his arse too?

MOTHER
...

FATHER
... Please, tell me it's never happened!

MOTHER
It's none of your business.

FATHER
What a sly little bastard, I underestimated him!

MOTHER
Shut it. He's not well.

FATHER
Neither am I, but I don't let you wipe my arse.

MOTHER
You wouldn't understand. Your mother never loved you.

FATHER
Yes, well, we've seen what yours does; instead of telling him to go to hell, she's all over him: "What's wrong, my love? What's upset you? Have you shit your pants? It doesn't matter, here, let me clean you up". Thanks very much – I can do without that kind of love.

MOTHER

And what else was she supposed to do? Do you have any better ideas?

FATHER

The best thing you can do with people like that is let them fall on their face. Or even better, to shoot them between the eyes and put them out of their misery.

MOTHER

And you, who is going to put you out of your misery?

FATHER

It's not going to happen to me. I won't let my son become like him.

MOTHER

Oh really? And what will you do?

FATHER

Absolutely nothing!

MOTHER

I shouldn't have asked.

FATHER

Let him work up a bit of a sweat and then you'll see.

MOTHER

Forget it – I don't want to know.

FATHER

Why won't you just listen to me for once? I know a thing or two.

MOTHER

And you know what the boy needs?

FATHER

(Whispering.) And who does know? The doctor?

MOTHER

...

FATHER
Do you want him to turn out like your brother?

MOTHER
There's worse than my brother.

FATHER
Really? Is there?

MOTHER
Are calling him crazy now?

FATHER
Oh yes, I'm sorry – I forgot. I'm the crazy one.

MOTHER
No-one is crazy here, not you, not me, not my brother, not the boy. No-one.

FATHER
If that's the case, what do we need the doctor for?

MOTHER
… I'm not sure/

FATHER
We've tried everything else. What have we got to lose?

MOTHER
… I don't know.

FATHER
That's what my mother did – she let me fall on my face. I may not be the best person in the world, but at least no-one wipes my arse for me.

MOTHER
Yes, but she did it out of meanness.

FATHER
And we'll do it out of kindness.

> Pause.

MOTHER
What about the doctor?

FATHER
Leave him to me.

2

The living room.

FATHER
So, we won't be needing you anymore.

DOCTOR
… I don't recommend it.

FATHER
(Taking his hand out of his pocket.) What do I owe you?

DOCTOR
Just listen to me for a moment – therapy is at a very critical point.

FATHER
Doctor, I am not my wife, you know.

DOCTOR
… And how am I supposed to take that?

FATHER
I don't know. Take it any way you want.

DOCTOR
In other words, you're telling me that you don't trust me!

FATHER
In other words and in so many words.

DOCTOR
Why did you call me in the first place then?

FATHER
I did it as a favour to my wife.

DOCTOR
What about doing your son a favour?

Pause.

DOCTOR
Are you worried about her?

FATHER
Every time she walks into that room...

DOCTOR
What exactly are you afraid of?

FATHER
That she'll never leave it again.

DOCTOR
But she does leave it eventually...doesn't she?

FATHER
Each time there's less of her... Still, that's what mothers are like, aren't they?

DOCTOR
Not all of them.

FATHER
True, there are also those that leave others alone.

DOCTOR
Was yours like that?

Pause.

FATHER
I should have known... She can't keep her filthy mouth shut.

DOCTOR
You don't understand – I heard you earlier.

FATHER
Just a minute – you were eavesdropping?!

DOCTOR
It's not like I had a choice.

FATHER
Listen to him – you should have stuck your fingers in your ears.

DOCTOR
You shouldn't have been shouting.

FATHER
Don't take that tone with me.

DOCTOR
You started it.

FATHER
I'm paying!

    Pause.

DOCTOR
Your son talked to me, you know.

FATHER
... Now you remember?!

DOCTOR
He asked me not to tell anyone.

FATHER
What the hell am I paying you for?

DOCTOR
I didn't want to betray his trust.

FATHER
You just did.

DOCTOR
I had to. The priorities have changed.

FATHER
Yes, now it could cost you.

DOCTOR
You should know that terminating therapy at this point could have some serious consequences.

FATHER
Right, I'll keep that in mind.

DOCTOR
I hope you know you're making a mistake.

FATHER
Will one more make any difference?

DOCTOR
And what if I'm right?

FATHER
I'll give you a call.

　　Pause.

DOCTOR
Fine – I need a final session with him.

FATHER
Why?

DOCTOR
To salvage whatever I can.

FATHER
How much will that cost me?

DOCTOR
Nothing.

FATHER
Good. You know where his room is.

　　The doctor begins to leave.

FATHER
Doctor... Just out of curiosity. What did he say to you?

3

The parents' bedroom. FATHER is sitting on the bed. MOTHER enters carrying a tablecloth all bundled up.

FATHER
(Whispering.)... Is he asleep?

MOTHER
He seems to be.

FATHER
Thank God! *(Whispering.)* OK? Did you get them?

MOTHER opens the bundle. It is full of cutlery.

MOTHER
Everything, except for the butter knives.

FATHER
Are you crazy?!

MOTHER
I am not going to drag my entire kitchen into the bedroom every night.

FATHER
Didn't you hear what the doctor said? Do I have to remind you what he said?

MOTHER
Oh really? And since when do you agree with the doctor?

FATHER
What the hell is he doing holed up in his room for so many days? Can you tell me that?

MOTHER
Why don't you go and see?

FATHER
Are you sure you shut the door? I didn't hear the key turn.

MOTHER
Don't change the subject. We have to talk to him.

FATHER
You talk to him!

Pause.

MOTHER
What shall we do then? Do you have any ideas?

FATHER
(Quietly.) I don't know…call the police maybe?

MOTHER
Are you out of your mind? And what would we tell them?

FATHER
The truth – that they should put him in a loony bin, somewhere.

MOTHER
It's us they'll put in the loony bin.

FATHER
In either case, we'll be off the hook.

A knock at the door. FATHER takes a kitchen knife from the bundle.

MOTHER
Now what are you doing?!

FATHER
(Whispering.) I'm being cautious.

MOTHER
Just put that down for god's sake

She moves towards the door.

FATHER
Where are you going?

MOTHER
To see what the boy wants.

FATHER
Stay where you are!

MOTHER
(Shaking her head.) You see what you've become?

FATHER
Shhhh *(He listens.)* No, it's just the wind.

SON
(From outside.) Mama?

MOTHER
… He's talking!!

FATHER
(Whispering.) What does he want?

MOTHER
It's us he wants, you idiot, he wants us.

FATHER
What for?

SON
Dad?

FATHER
(Whispering.) Don't open the door.

MOTHER
How can you stand it? How long is it since you last heard his voice?

SON
Mama, are you there?

She moves towards the door.

FATHER
(Whispering.) I said don't open it.

MOTHER
(Whispering.) You're afraid of your own child?

FATHER
(Whispering.) That thing out there is not our child.

MOTHER
(Shaking her head.)... Why do I even bother talking to you?

She moves towards the door.

FATHER
(Whispering.) For god's sake. Am I the only sane person in here?

MOTHER opens the door. She leaves the room.

Don't, Dooon't...

MOTHER
(From outside the room.) My darling boy...are you there?

Quiet.

Then footsteps.

FATHER is at the ready.

MOTHER returns to the room holding a scrap of paper.

MOTHER
(Reading.) "There's no milk in the fridge. Or any bread."
You see how you over-react.

FATHER
He's poking fun at us as well.

MOTHER
In case you didn't get it, he's decided to speak to us!

FATHER gets up and closes the door.

FATHER
(Quietly.) He's after something.

MOTHER
What he wants is to eat.

FATHER
I have a bad feeling about all this.

MOTHER
Fine – I'm going to prepare something for him.

FATHER
What are you doing?

MOTHER
What do you want me to do? Let him starve?

FATHER
We said that we would leave him alone. We agreed – didn't we?

MOTHER
That was before. Now he's asking for help.

FATHER
What makes you think that?

MOTHER
(*Showing the note.*) It doesn't take a genius to figure it out –
He says so here "there's no milk".

FATHER
What does he mean there's no milk? There was a whole carton
in the fridge.

MOTHER
He might have drunk it, it might have gone bad.

FATHER
How could he have finished it? I bought it the day before
yesterday.

MOTHER
It wasn't the day before yesterday.

FATHER
Don't you get it, he wants to lure us out of the room.

MOTHER
(*Shaking her head.*) You're pathetic.

FATHER
Let's not take that risk just yet.

MOTHER
Get out of my sight.

FATHER
Fine! Whatever you like... I'm calling the doctor.

MOTHER
Oh really?... For whom?

4

The SON's room.

The DOCTOR is sitting opposite the SON. The parents are in the background.

DOCTOR
. Your parents are ready to speak to you. They want to know what is worrying you...if there is some way of helping you...they're here for you, this time they're prepared to do anything at all...

Whispering in the background.

DOCTOR
They're here, and they're going to stay here...for as long as necessary, you take all the time you need, they have the patience...

Whispering in the background.

DOCTOR
The only thing they want is for you to know that your problem is their problem, but they don't know how to make you understand that, perhaps they haven't found the right way to show you...

MOTHER
(Whispers to FATHER.) Shut up, for God's sake.

The DOCTOR throws them a warning glance.

DOCTOR
It's hard for them to change, you see, but the important thing is that they want to try, they're committed to that...they're prepared to admit their mistakes and to do the best they can... How does that seem to you as a first step?...

FATHER

(From the background.) As if he's going to speak!

DOCTOR

(To the parents.) Perhaps you'd like to say something?...
If there's something you'd like to say, now is the right time.

FATHER

(To MOTHER.)... Why are you looking at me? You are the one
who wanted to talk to him – Go on, go ahead.

DOCTOR

Come on, there's no reason to hold back – come closer...
Come on, this is your chance.

MOTHER

You come too...

FATHER

In a little while...don't glare at me – I have my reasons.

*MOTHER shakes her head and approaches the SON. She sits
by him.*

DOCTOR

You can speak to him; don't be afraid, he doesn't bite.

FATHER

Right...

MOTHER

... Your father and I want to know what's happening with you...

She looks at the DOCTOR for assurance.

If we did something wrong, don't be shy – tell us and we'll
admit to it, if you want us to pay for it...

FATHER

Listen to what she's saying – that's right, put ideas into his
head now.

MOTHER

... Don't listen to your father, don't forget that he grew up with
a very bad person, he doesn't know how to deal with this kind

of thing, he thinks that it'll be the end of the world if he admits to a mistake, and yet even he is here for you...he loves you, you know... *(To the FATHER.)* isn't that right?... Tell him.

FATHER
(From the background.) Tell him what?!

MOTHER
... Tell him that you love him.

FATHER
... Just like that, out of the blue?

MOTHER
Tell him!!

FATHER
... OK – I love you, son.

MOTHER
And we will always do, whatever happens, even if you tell us you want to kill us/

FATHER
(To MOTHER.) Have you gone mad? What on earth are you saying?

MOTHER
Because if that's what it takes, go ahead, do it – we are standing right here in front of you /telling you to do whatever you think is right.

FATHER
(To the DOCTOR.)...tell her to shut up.

MOTHER
Because I am sick and tired of not knowing what's going on, I'm tired of it...just do whatever you think best.

   MOTHER appears with a kitchen knife.

   And you can start with me.

DOCTOR
(To MOTHER.) Please, control yourself. You're not helping the situation.

FATHER

(To the DOCTOR.)... What are you standing looking at her for? Take it away from her, for Heaven's sake. (To MOTHER.) Put it down, put it down.

MOTHER

Take it, let's not waste any time, me first.

FATHER

What are you doing? For Heaven's sake... (To the DOCTOR.) Take the knife away from her now, you poor excuse for a doctor.

DOCTOR

(To MOTHER.) Please put it down – try to stay calm.

MOTHER

I can't bear any more calmness, I can't – I'm tired of it.

    The DOCTOR approaches MOTHER.

DOCTOR

No-one said it was easy. For the moment, let's all try to stay calm...let's all take a deep breath – I think we all need it... come on, everyone please take a deep, deep breath.

    MOTHER takes short, irregular breaths.

Why don't you let me hold that for a bit, eh?

FATHER

(To MOTHER.) Go on, give it to him. That's enough of that.

DOCTOR

Please, sir.

FATHER

(To MOTHER.) So tell me what you think you achieved with your hysterics?

DOCTOR

Please. You're making things worse.

FATHER
I'm making them worse? She put the knife in his hand and I'm the one making things worse?

MOTHER
Yes, everything is my fault – I admit it. But do you know something? You are not my fault. You are no-one's fault. Not even your mother's. She is who she is – she doesn't pretend to be a saint. You are the bad person. Its only god's fault that you are what you are.

FATHER
Yes, let's blame everything on god now.

MOTHER
Shut up.

FATHER
Doctor, you can see who needs your help.

MOTHER
Shut up right now.

FATHER
Or what?!

MOTHER
Go to Hell.

FATHER
Thanks to you, I am already there!

She attacks the FATHER with the knife.

DOCTOR steps between them.

She stabs him.

He grabs his wound.

MOTHER pulls out the knife.

DOCTOR falls to the ground.

FATHER
… What have you done?!

MOTHER
I didn't mean to.

FATHER
How the Hell did that happen?

MOTHER
He stepped between us.

FATHER
Just as well – you would have killed me.

MOTHER
Oh my God… What have I done?

FATHER
Give me that thing.

> *He approaches her cautiously.*

> Give me that…careful now, eh?

> *He takes the knife. The DOCTOR coughs once.*

MOTHER
He's alive?!

> *FATHER approaches the DOCTOR. He observes.*

FATHER
I'm not sure.

MOTHER
He just coughed – didn't you hear him?

FATHER
It may have been his last gasp.

> *He coughs again.*

MOTHER
He's alive!!

FATHER
(*To himself.*) And this is where we get thrown in jail.

> *MOTHER kneels in front of the DOCTOR.*

267

MOTHER
Doctor, can you hear me? Everything will be all right. Don't worry, I'll call for help.

FATHER
You aren't calling anyone.

MOTHER
But he's alive.

FATHER
(Whispering.) He's dead all right. He just hasn't realized it yet.

MOTHER
He'll make it.

FATHER
And we'll get life imprisonment.

MOTHER
You didn't do anything.

FATHER
You're not taking the boy into account, are you? Where will he go? Who's going to take care of him, eh?

    The DOCTOR coughs again.

MOTHER
I can't leave him like this.

    She gets up. FATHER grabs her by the shoulders.

FATHER
Wait a minute. Just a little bit longer.

MOTHER
No, I'm calling an ambulance.

    She moves towards the exit.

FATHER
Wait.

He kneels and, with his eyes closed, stabs the DOCTOR very quickly.

Listen to me – wait – wait – can't you – wait?

DOCTOR dies.

There, are you satisfied now?

MOTHER
... Why?!

FATHER
You gave me no choice.

Pause.

FATHER
Don't sit there.

He drops the knife. He grabs the DOCTOR by the hands.

Grab his legs. Come on, don't just stand there.

MOTHER
(In a quiet voice.) ... The boy is watching us.

FATHER
(In a quiet voice.) Who do you think we're doing this for? Now grab the legs.

MOTHER grabs the DOCTOR by the feet.

And a one, and a two, and a three, go...

They lift him. They look at each other. He signals to her.

Into the bathroom.

They go out.

SON remains alone in the room.

He looks at the knife.

They can be heard from the bathroom.

FATHER
... Put his legs over there...like that – and I'll/

MOTHER
Be careful – his head.

FATHER
Why? You think it'll hurt him?... There we are.

MOTHER
... And now what?

FATHER
I think we need lime.

MOTHER
What? What for?

FATHER
It helps the rotting process – so they say.

MOTHER
Are you sure?

FATHER
Well, this is the first time it has happened to me, you know.

MOTHER
And where are we going to find lime at this hour?

FATHER
I don't know – Call your mother.

MOTHER
No, I'm not mixing my mother up in this.

FATHER
Would you rather I call mine?

They return back to the living room.

MOTHER
...isn't there some other way?

FATHER
Like what? Throwing the doctor out of the window?

MOTHER
No, not my mother – she'll drop dead on the spot.

FATHER
She won't, she'll have no problem with it.

MOTHER
She won't do it.

FATHER
She'll do it for you.

MOTHER
I don't think so.

FATHER
She wipes you brother's arse, doesn't she?

MOTHER
No, forget about it.

FATHER
Do you have a better idea?

> *He looks at his son who is looking at the knife. He picks up the knife from the floor.*

MOTHER
… What about you? Why don't you go and get it?

FATHER
Are you mad? And leave you here alone? I'm not leaving you alone.

MOTHER
Why not?

FATHER
No way. You might do something stupid again.

MOTHER
Oh God, how can I have done it?

FATHER
Leave God out of it and pick up the phone.

MOTHER
What shall I tell her?

FATHER
Just tell her that you need a sack of limes.

He moves towards the bathroom.

MOTHER
And what if she asks me what I want it for?

FATHER
I don't know; tell her it's for the garden, for repairs...
Use your brain.

MOTHER
She'll know there's something funny going on.

FATHER
Listen to me. Just take a deep breath and say: Mum, do you
have a spare sack of limes?

5

The living room.

*MOTHER is next to the door. FATHER is standing a little further
away.*

GRANDMOTHER enters holding her handbag.

GRANDMOTHER
(Sniffing the air.) Pfff...for goodness sake – the house stinks.
How'd you manage to get it smelling like this?

The parents look at each other.

What's wrong with you? Why don't you say something?

They look at each other.

... Has something happened to the boy?

MOTHER
No, Mama, why would you think that?

GRANDMOTHER
Thank god... *(She sits.)* And what about you lot?

FATHER
What about us?

MOTHER
We're fine, Mama.

GRANDMOTHER
(To FATHER.) What have you done to her again?

FATHER
Me? /

GRANDMOTHER
Carrion!

FATHER
Look, I'm really not in the mood.

> *GRANDMOTHER stands up, holding her bag.*

GRANDMOTHER
(Sniffing the air.) Where is it coming from? Is it in here?

She searches the room, following the smell. MOTHER follows her.

MOTHER
Come on, Mama, it's nothing.

GRANDMOTHER
What do you mean nothing? It stinks of carrion.

MOTHER
The shutters are closed – that's why.

GRANDMOTHER
Why don't you open them?

MOTHER
Because of the boy.

GRANDMOTHER
Why? Is he allergic to the sun?

MOTHER
Just to be sure...that he doesn't get any funny ideas.

GRANDMOTHER
What's this rubbish you're talking now? Open a window before I keel over.

FATHER
Right, let's go.

GRANDMOTHER
Go where?

FATHER
Downstairs – so you can give me the lime?

GRANDMOTHER
What do you want lime for? At least tell me that.

FATHER
Some other time.

GRANDMOTHER
And why did you make me lug it over here, an old woman like me?

FATHER
Are you going to give it to me or not?

She looks at them suspiciously.

GRANDMOTHER
(Sniffing.) Is it coming from the kitchen?

MOTHER
... Yes, from the kitchen.

GRANDMOTHER
Why are you taking so long to reply? What is it?

MOTHER
Nothing, some rotten fruit. We were about to throw it out.

GRANDMOTHER
There's no way that smell comes from fruit. I smell carrion,
I tell you.

She moves towards the kitchen. MOTHER follows her.

MOTHER
…it's probably a mouse.

GRANDMOTHER
A stench like that? It can't possibly be just one.

She puts down her handbag and they leave the room.

It must be a whole extended family.

FATHER hears them shouting.

MOTHER
Leave it, I'll do it.

GRANDMOTHER
It's a bit late for that. Bring the broom.

MOTHER
Mama, it's my house.

GRANDMOTHER
Yes, but I bought it for you. And from what I remember there
was no stench of carrion then – do you know what could
happen if you have carrion in the house?…

MOTHER
I know, Mama, I know.

GRANDMOTHER
So, come on, bring me the broom.

MOTHER
I said I'll do it.

GRANDMOTHER
When?!

MOTHER
As soon as you let me, Mama, just as soon as you let me.

GRANDMOTHER
... I don't understand you people – I give up.

They return to the room.

If you don't want me under your feet, why did you call me over?

FATHER takes the handbag.

FATHER
Are we off?

GRANDMOTHER
With pleasure – I'll just pop in and see the boy and then I'll get out of your way.

FATHER
You probably shouldn't!

GRANDMOTHER
What are you talking about? Who says so?

FATHER
... The doctor.

GRANDMOTHER
The doctor?!!

MOTHER
Yes. The doctor said so.

GRANDMOTHER
Who do you mean? The doctor who's achieved absolutely nothing all this time?

FATHER
He's the one we're stuck with – what do you want us to do about it?

GRANDMOTHER
Get rid of him, while you can. If you don't, you deserve whatever you get.

FATHER holds out the handbag.

FATHER
Are we off then?

GRANDMOTHER grabs her handbag, annoyed.

GRANDMOTHER
Can't a grandmother see her grandson? Where else could that happen? These doctors should be burned at the stake.

They make as though to leave. GRANDMOTHER stops suddenly. She gives the handbag back to FATHER.

GRANDMOTHER
Give me a minute. I have to go to the toilet.

MOTHER
Now?

GRANDMOTHER
I have to. All thanks to you for upsetting me.

She moves towards the bathroom. They obstruct her.

MOTHER
What about my brother?

GRANDMOTHER
What about your brother?

MOTHER
Have you left him on his own?

GRANDMOTHER
It's not the first time.

MOTHER
You never leave him alone.

GRANDMOTHER
This is not the time for spite and jealousy, you know.

MOTHER
Aren't you worried?

GRANDMOTHER
(Stroking her cheek.)... I worry about you, too, you know.

She goes to move forward. The MOTHER obstructs her.

How much longer are we going to carry on like this, eh? Let me go to the toilet, dear – for goodness sake.

FATHER
You don't want to see that.

GRANDMOTHER
See what?

MOTHER
Nothing – there's nothing to see.

GRANDMOTHER
... Will you tell me what's going on?

MOTHER
Nothing's going on, Mama. Why do you say that?

GRANDMOTHER
... You're hiding something from me, aren't you?

She moves towards the bathroom. MOTHER gets in her way.

GRANDMOTHER
Let me through.

MOTHER
No – it's for your own good.

GRANDMOTHER
What rubbish, you telling me what's for my own good!

FATHER
Let her go.

MOTHER shakes her head.

She asked for it.

MOTHER steps aside. GRANDMOTHER looks at them attentively.

GRANDMOTHER
I think that others are in need of a doctor around here – not the boy.

She goes into the bathroom. After a short while she comes out again. She looks at them.

Who is he?!

FATHER
… The doctor.

GRANDMOTHER
(To FATHER.) And why did you kill the doctor?

FATHER
Me?

GRANDMOTHER
You know you have to give yourself up.

FATHER
I don't have to do anything.

GRANDMOTHER
Wasn't it you who killed him?

FATHER
I hate to disappoint you.

GRANDMOTHER looks at her daughter. MOTHER lowers her gaze.

GRANDMOTHER
… Impossible!

FATHER
Not what you expected?

MOTHER begins to sob. GRANDMOTHER approaches her.

GRANDMOTHER
Don't cry. We'll deal with it. Just stop crying.

FATHER
What? Aren't we going to call the cops now?

GRANDMOTHER
Are you out of your mind?

FATHER
Why not? Because she's your daughter?

GRANDMOTHER
Yes, because she's my daughter.

FATHER
You are unbelievable!

GRANDMOTHER
Now that I think of it, I might call them and tell them that you did it.

FATHER
Oh really? Are you sure?

GRANDMOTHER
As God is my witness.

FATHER
Just try it.

GRANDMOTHER
You don't scare me.

MOTHER
Stop it!

She makes as though to leave.

GRANDMOTHER
Where do you think you are going now?

MOTHER
I'm calling the police. This has to end.

GRANDMOTHER
Stay where you are.

MOTHER
This can't go on.

GRANDMOTHER
Don't move an inch, I said.

FATHER
I never expected to say it, but, at last, a sensible person.

MOTHER hesitates.

MOTHER
... No. It's not right.

She makes as though to leave. GRANDMOTHER grabs her.

GRANDMOTHER
He's dead. Gone, finished. You can't do anything about that. If only you could, but... What can we do? And it's not as though you did it on purpose. You didn't do it on purpose, did you?

MOTHER shakes her head.

What's important now is your family.

MOTHER
What about his family?

GRANDMOTHER
We don't have to destroy two families. And we surely don't need to be buried with him.

GRANDMOTHER grabs her and shakes her.

Do you want to go to jail? And not ever see your child again? – Is that what you want? Are you that selfish? Can't you think of anyone other than yourself?

FATHER
Your mother's right.

GRANDMOTHER
(To FATHER.) Lime. We need lime.

FATHER
Yes, that's what I said.

GRANDMOTHER
And who's going to bring it up? Me?

FATHER shakes his head in annoyance and leaves.

What about the boy? Where was he? Was he there? Did he see everything?

6

The SON's room.

SON is sitting on the bed.

Someone knocks on the door.

GRANDMOTHER
(From outside.) Sweetheart? It's Granny. Can I come in?

She enters.

How's my little boy?

SON
I'm killing time.

GRANDMOTHER
There are worse things. Your mother killed the doctor.

SON
It was bound to happen one day.

GRANDMOTHER
Why do you say that?... Did he do something to you?

SON
The man just did his job.

GRANDMOTHER
And?

SON
Therapy failed!

GRANDMOTHER
You can tell me, my boy. What did he do to you? Anything he shouldn't have?

SON
You're dying of curiosity, aren't you?

GRANDMOTHER
My daughter killed someone, and I want to know why.

SON
Don't worry. She didn't do it by herself.

GRANDMOTHER
… Your father?

SON
What? Don't you think he's capable of it?

GRANDMOTHER
The coward – he blamed it all on your mother.

SON
She started it and he finished him off.

She approaches him.

GRANDMOTHER
My poor boy, what a thing to happen before your very eyes…

She strokes and arranges his hair.

SON
You should have seen them – it was as if they'd been at it for years.

GRANDMOTHER
Hush – it's not funny.

Pause.

GRANDMOTHER
Is that your stomach rumbling?

He nods his head.

Some milk? Would you like milk? Shall I bring you a glass?

SON
There's no milk. It's finished.

GRANDMOTHER
Finished?

SON
There's no bread either.

She takes his face in her hands. She looks at him with concern.

GRANDMOTHER
Tell me the truth, my boy... How long is it since your mother's cooked food for the family?

SON
She doesn't have the time.

GRANDMOTHER
What the hell does she have to do that leaves her no time to cook?

SON
How should I know? She kills people.

GRANDMOTHER
Stop that. It's not funny... When did you last eat?

SON
Days... I can't remember how many.

GRANDMOTHER
Things have got completely out of hand... This is not a good place for you.

She leaves.

7

The parents' bedroom.

The parents are in the room. A knock at the door. They are startled and afraid. Someone tries to open the door. It is locked.

GRANDMOTHER
(From outside.) Open the door, for goodness sake – it's me.

    MOTHER opens the door. GRANDMOTHER enters.

    What on earth is wrong with you? Why have you locked the door?

FATHER
We have our reasons.

GRANDMOTHER
(Sighs.) Oh, my poor child.

MOTHER
How is he?

GRANDMOTHER
How do you think he is?

MOTHER
Did he talk to you at all?

GRANDMOTHER
Better he hadn't opened his mouth.

MOTHER
What did he say?

GRANDMOTHER
Do you realize how long it's been since he's had anything to eat?

MOTHER
…

GRANDMOTHER
Why aren't you feeding him?

FATHER
He's a big boy. If he's hungry he can go and cook himself something.

GRANDMOTHER
Cook what? There's nothing in the fridge.

FATHER
He's lying. There's a bottle of milk and a loaf of sliced bread.

GRANDMOTHER
The bottle is empty and the bread is mouldy.

FATHER
Mouldy, my arse. I put it in the fridge myself.

GRANDMOTHER
When?

FATHER
I went shopping a few days ago. *(To MOTHER.)* When was it that I went shopping?

MOTHER
It wasn't a few days ago.

FATHER
Go and see if you don't believe me.

GRANDMOTHER
I've just come from the kitchen/ if you can call it a kitchen. There's nothing in it…

   Pause

GRANDMOTHER
(To MOTHER.) Why haven't you been shopping?

MOTHER
Mama, I just killed a man.

GRANDMOTHER
And you thought you'd do away with the boy too, did you?

FATHER

The world's falling apart and we're talking about/

GRANDMOTHER

What do you two eat? That's what I'd like to know.

FATHER

Is this the time to be talking about food?

GRANDMOTHER

Well, we have to start somewhere if we're going to make any sense of what's going on.

FATHER

We don't have the time for this.

GRANDMOTHER

Of course not, given the mess you've made...

FATHER

... Excuse me?

GRANDMOTHER

Do you want me to spell it out?

FATHER

Watch your tongue.

GRANDMOTHER

Why, do you think you might kill me too, now?

FATHER

I didn't kill anyone, OK?

GRANDMOTHER

Oh, I can't imagine you didn't have a hand in it.

FATHER

... Did he tell you? *(To MOTHER.)* He told her.

GRANDMOTHER

Are you completely out of your minds? You killed the doctor in front of his eyes?

FATHER
That was not our intention, you know/

MOTHER
Wrong place, wrong time…

GRANDMOTHER
That's an understatement. Now, here's what's going to happen. Since you killed the doctor, you'll keep him company until he rots. The boy, however, had nothing to do with it. So the boy is coming with me.

FATHER
Be my guest.

GRANDMOTHER
I'm glad we agree.

MOTHER
No.

GRANDMOTHER
I didn't ask you.

MOTHER
The boy will stay here, with us. In his own house.

GRANDMOTHER
Why? So you can set a good example for him?

MOTHER
We did it for him.

GRANDMOTHER
You've made every possible mistake. That's what you did.

FATHER
Yes, we've seen how well you've done.

GRANDMOTHER
What do you mean?

FATHER
You don't want me to start on your son.

GRANDMOTHER
Don't even mention my son, or as God is my witness...

FATHER
... Go on, take him – be my guest. That way you'll have two arses to wipe. And then there will be no stopping you.

GRANDMOTHER
(To MOTHER.) Do you hear him? Do you hear what he's saying about your family?

MOTHER
He and the boy are my family.

GRANDMOTHER
Him you can keep, but forget about the boy.

MOTHER
I'll pretend I didn't hear that.

GRANDMOTHER
Pretend whatever you like. I'm taking the boy with me.

MOTHER
No!

GRANDMOTHER
In that case I'll go to the police.

FATHER
(To MOTHER.) Let her take him, he'll be fine. She's his grandmother after all.

MOTHER
And I'm his mother.

GRANDMOTHER
Let's not go there – You're not exactly the perfect mother.

MOTHER
You know what they say: Like mother like daughter.

GRANDMOTHER slaps her. MOTHER slaps her back.

MOTHER
I'm sorry.

GRANDMOTHER
Get out of my sight.

She begins to move past her. MOTHER catches hold of her.

MOTHER
Mama, I'm sorry. I didn't mean it.

GRANDMOTHER
Take your filthy hands off me. *(Shrieking.)* Don't touch me I said.

She tries to move past. MOTHER gets in her way.

MOTHER
Please…

GRANDMOTHER
I won't say it again – get out of my way.

MOTHER
… I can't.

GRANDMOTHER
I said, get out of my way.

GRANDMOTHER pulls her by the hair.

MOTHER
Let me go, let go.

FATHER
Let her go, let her go, you old cow.

The FATHER tries to separate them.

MOTHER
Mama…you're hurting me. Let me go, Mama…

GRANDMOTHER
Don't ever call me that again. I curse the day that I brought you into the world.

FATHER pushes GRANDMOTHER violently. He shoves her against the wall. She grabs her breast. She finds herself on the floor. MOTHER kneels beside her.

MOTHER
Mama? Are you all right?... Mama?

She takes her in her arms.

... Say something – please...

GRANDMOTHER raises herself slightly, trying to catch her breath. She falls back into her daughter's arms.

MOTHER
Mama?... Mama?

Silence.

FATHER
... Please don't tell me she's...

Pause.

FATHER
Shit, shit and more shit.

The MOTHER looks at him.

Don't look at me like that. I didn't do anything. I only...

MOTHER
(Drained.) You've killed her.

FATHER
What was I supposed to do? She was going to take the boy.

MOTHER
Why didn't I let her? What difference would it have made if she'd taken him?

FATHER
That's what I said, but you wouldn't listen.

MOTHER
What shall I do?... How am I going to tell my brother?

FATHER grabs GRANDMOTHER by the feet.

FATHER
Come on, grab her.

MOTHER
What are you doing?

FATHER
Stop looking at me like that – we've done it before. Come on now, grab her hands.

MOTHER looks at the corpse as if hypnotized.

Don't look. Don't look, I tell you.

MOTHER begins to cry.

No, not now, please. Come on, sweetheart...please.

FATHER lets go of GRANDMOTHER's feet. He approaches MOTHER.

FATHER
(Gently.) Come on. It's all right. Leave her, leave her to me.

MOTHER
I didn't do it on purpose.

FATHER
I know – an ill-starred day. Come on, don't give up now. I need you to be strong.

MOTHER
Mama...

FATHER
Don't...don't

The MOTHER collapses.

MOTHER
Mama, what have I done?

FATHER
For God's sake, listen to me.

He grabs her by the shoulders.

Listen to me. Whatever's happened has happened, there's no going back – Not my words, it was your mother who said it.

MOTHER
As if she knew...

FATHER
(Tenderly.) Think of the boy. Don't give up on him.

MOTHER
The boy...

FATHER
Aren't we doing all this for him, eh? Come on now. Grab that end. Come on...

They pick up the GRANDMOTHER. They leave. They can be heard from the bathroom.

MOTHER
Oh my God.

FATHER
Don't – be careful.

MOTHER
I'm going to faint.

FATHER
Hold on, hold on... Good girl. A little bit further... That's it. There we are.

They return quickly from the bathroom. They shut the door. They take deep breaths.

MOTHER
... We'll never get rid of that smell, will we?

FATHER
... We need lime.

MOTHER
The whole house stinks.

FATHER
Two or three sacks would do it.

MOTHER
That's our punishment.

FATHER
What shall I do? Shall I burn the damned thing?

MOTHER
This is impossible, we have to get them out of here – bury them.

FATHER
Why don't you call the police while you're at it?

MOTHER
Don't think I haven't thought of it.

FATHER
Just accept it – they're not going anywhere until they've rotted to the bone!

MOTHER
And what are we going to do until then? Sit around and watch?

FATHER
… That's our punishment.

Pause.

MOTHER
And the boy?… How are we going to tell the boy?

They sigh.

8

The SON's room.

SON is on the bed. MOTHER is sitting next to him. FATHER is standing.

SON
Was it you who killed her?

MOTHER
... Why on earth would you say that?

SON
You've done it before – that's why.

MOTHER
It was an accident...

SON
And now? It's my turn, isn't it?

MOTHER
What are you talking about, darling?

SON
Well, you've done away with everyone else.

FATHER
She said it was an accident – what don't you understand?

Pause.

SON
Fine. *(To MOTHER.)* Did you get any bread?

She shakes her head.

SON
Milk?

MOTHER
... No!

SON
So what did you come here for?

MOTHER goes to embrace the SON.

MOTHER
I'm sorry, darling.

He obstructs her.

SON
I get it... It's my turn now. You're going to starve me to death.
It will be easier this way.

FATHER
Do you hear that? That's the kind of person your son is.

MOTHER
I won't tell you who he reminds me of... *(To the SON.)* My boy, listen to me. I am sure that somewhere deep inside you can hear me and understand what I'm saying. You know that I am your mother and that the only thing I want is what is best for you. I'll go to the bakery – I promise. As soon as I can. Don't worry, we'll sort all this out and then I'll go shopping.

SON
Don't you worry either; I will sort things out too. I'll sort things out for sure.

FATHER
What does he mean by that? Is he threatening us? Eh, is he threatening us?

9

The parents' bedroom.

FATHER is sitting on the bed. MOTHER, on all fours, is counting the cutlery.

MOTHER
Forks, knives, spoons...they're all here.

FATHER
Are you sure?

MOTHER
Don't worry/

FATHER
What do you mean don't worry? Weren't you there? Didn't you hear what he said – "I'll sort things out".

MOTHER
He's got bigger problems than us right now, you know.

FATHER
You poor thing. You are completely clueless.

MOTHER
What I am is tired.

FATHER
And you think I'm not?

MOTHER
So why don't you go to sleep?

FATHER
It's not that easy, you know!

MOTHER
We don't have a lot of choice.

FATHER
Where will all this end? All that's left is for us to kill each other.

MOTHER
That won't happen.

FATHER
I'm not so sure any more.

MOTHER
(In a quiet voice.) Me neither…

FATHER
On the other hand, we might be lucky and he'll kill us off first.

MOTHER
He doesn't want to kill us. He's just hungry.

FATHER
Well, why doesn't he eat, so that we can all relax, eh?

MOTHER
There's no food in the house – When are you going to take that in?

FATHER
What the hell do we eat then?

MOTHER
Good question – what do we eat?

FATHER
... Wait a minute – when did we last eat? The day before yesterday, wasn't it?

MOTHER
I don't know. What day was the day before yesterday?

FATHER
Wasn't it Tuesday?... What day was it? Wednesday?

MOTHER
I don't remember.

FATHER
Wait – It can't be... It was...

MOTHER
You don't remember either.

FATHER
(Holding his head.) That's it, I've lost it.

MOTHER
What does it matter anymore? The way things stand; it's probably just as well.

    She begins to cry. He moves to embrace her. She moves away.

MOTHER
God, you stink.

FATHER
Why? Do you think you smell like a rose garden?

    MOTHER sniffs her clothes.

MOTHER
Oh my God. How long is it since we've washed?

FATHER
Probably as long as it is since we've eaten.

MOTHER
Why didn't you say anything?

FATHER
Say what?

MOTHER
You stink – take a bath.

FATHER
How? They haven't decomposed yet.

MOTHER
Yet?!

FATHER
Yes, I have to throw in some more lime.

MOTHER
What are you waiting for then? Go and throw more in.

FATHER
We don't have any more.

MOTHER
Why not?

FATHER
We didn't reckon on your mother.

> *Pause.*

MOTHER
So be it – I really don't care.

> *She begins to take off her clothes in frenzy.*

There's nothing I can do, not for my mother, not for my son
– not for anyone...

> *She is naked.*

A warm bath, that's the only thing...

> *He watches her. She looks at him.*

... What are you looking at?!

FATHER
Nothing.

MOTHER
What do you mean nothing?! I can see you.

FATHER
It's been such a long time…

MOTHER
Really? Is that what you're thinking right now?

FATHER
I can't remember when I last saw you like this.

MOTHER
And you've got a hard-on?

FATHER
Is there anything wrong with that?

MOTHER
This is hardly the time…!

FATHER
I didn't do it on purpose. It just happened.

MOTHER
There's something wrong with you.

FATHER
Do you think I don't know that?

MOTHER
The sky is falling here, and you're thinking about/

FATHER
I stopped thinking, several days ago.

> He approaches her.

My brain isn't working anymore.

> He embraces her. He tries to kiss her.

MOTHER
No – I'm covered in blood, I stink.

FATHER
It doesn't matter. I'm used to it.

MOTHER
No...not like this.

FATHER
Fine. I'll go and run the bath.

MOTHER
(*Tired.*) Thank you.

    He leaves her and exits. He returns immediately.

FATHER
(*Stunned.*) Where's the doctor?

MOTHER
...what?!

FATHER
He's not there.

MOTHER
What do you mean he's not there?

FATHER
He's disappeared.

MOTHER
How can that be?

FATHER
How should I know?

MOTHER
Did you look carefully?

FATHER
What do you think?

MOTHER
Where the hell could he have gone?

She begins to dress.

Could he have disintegrated?

FATHER
So fast? No way.

MOTHER
So where did he go then? He just vanished into thin air?

They look at one another uneasily and then rush out of the room.

10

The SON's room.

The DOCTOR's feet protrude from under the bed. FATHER is looking at the corpse. SON is sitting on the bed. MOTHER is standing next to him.

FATHER
How could you do it?

SON
I washed off the lime first.

FATHER
I just can't believe it. Can you believe this?

MOTHER
How could you, darling?

SON
I was hungry...

MOTHER
I told you I would go shopping.

SON
When? After I was dead?

MOTHER
My boy, you've eaten human flesh – do you understand that?

SON
You two killed him.

MOTHER
We did it for you!

SON
You should have gone to the bakery – It would have been a lot simpler.

FATHER hits himself on the head with his hand.

FATHER
For the love of God, let's get out of here.

MOTHER
And what will you do – eat your grandmother now?

SON
Grandma wouldn't have minded – If it was for my own good.

FATHER pulls her.

FATHER
Come on – Haven't you heard enough?

SON
What is it you want from me? To starve to death?

MOTHER
What do you blame us for? Tell me. What have we ever done to you?

SON
What about me? What have I ever done to you?

11

The SON's room.

SON is sleeping. The blankets tucked up to his neck.

His parents enter on their tiptoes. MOTHER approaches the bed. FATHER keeps his distance. They whisper.

FATHER
Is he asleep?

MOTHER
He seems restless.

> *MOTHER watches the SON.*

… His pillow is soaked.

> *FATHER approaches.*

He must be having a nightmare, poor love.

FATHER
The Doctor must have given him indigestion.

MOTHER
… I can't do it.

FATHER
Oh no – You're not going to back out this time.

> *SON talks in his sleep. They freeze. MOTHER observes him.*

MOTHER
… So much effort, such sacrifices – all gone to waste.

FATHER
We tried. It's just not worth it anymore.

MOTHER
We'd be leaving a child behind.

FATHER
(Intensely.) What do you want me to do? Pretend nothing has happened?

MOTHER
Shhhh.

FATHER
(Quietly.) That everything's fine? Like before?

MOTHER
… Let's give him another chance.

FATHER
I'd rather cut my own throat.

MOTHER

...

The FATHER brings out a knife.

FATHER

(Quietly.) Fine. Tell me – Who do you want me to stab? Myself
or him? I'll do whatever you want. Go on, tell me, because I'm
sick of this – Who? *(He puts the knife to his throat.)* Just say
the word and it'll be done.

MOTHER

... Give it here, give it to me.

She stretches out her hand.

FATHER

What do you want?

MOTHER

Give it to me – I'll do it.

*She takes the knife. She lifts it to stab the SON. She shuts her
eyes. Her hands tremble.*

MOTHER

I can't...

FATHER

Shhh.

MOTHER

(She collapses.) I can't. I can't do it.

He approaches her. He takes her hand.

FATHER

Together... We started this together – we'll end it the same way.

They raise the knife together. SON moves. They freeze.

FATHER

(Quietly.)... He's awake?!

*MOTHER looks carefully. She shakes her head. They raise the
knife again. There's a knock at the door.*

12

The SON's room.

SON and his UNCLE are sitting opposite one another. The parents are by the door, whispering.

FATHER
Go on, ask him.

MOTHER
... No.

FATHER
Ask.

MOTHER
Not now – Later.

FATHER
What later? There is no later.

SON
What are you whispering about over there?

MOTHER
Nothing...

> *FATHER clears his throat.*

A knife has gone missing.

SON
What knife?

MOTHER
It's just an ordinary knife – a kitchen knife. Have you seen it, dear?

SON
Nah.

> *Pause.*

MOTHER
Oh, and guess what. I've been shopping.

SON
... Are you sure?!

MOTHER
It was about time, don't you think?

SON
You cooked?!

MOTHER
The table is set and waiting for you.

SON
I'd have to see it to believe it.

MOTHER
Go on... Smell.

SON
I don't smell food.

FATHER
Are you sure you haven't seen it?

SON
What, the knife?

FATHER
Yes, the knife. Don't pretend you don't understand.

SON
... Don't worry, in case I find it you'll be the first to know.

MOTHER
Come on now, let's go and eat.

SON
OK, you first/

MOTHER
Now, my boy – while the food is still hot.

SON
Shall I wash my hands first?

MOTHER
It'll get cold.

SON
I could have washed them by now.

They remain motionless.

MOTHER
Don't be late though, will you?

She moves towards the door. FATHER stays put. She pulls him and they exit. SON approaches the door. He closes it carefully and sighs.

SON
(Quietly.) Can you believe it? It's as if nothing has happened... Do you know where I'd be if you hadn't arrived? In the bath with Grandma... What? They didn't tell you? Do you think what you can smell is Mum's cooking? ... As if nothing has happened. First they'll drive me crazy and then they'll do away with me... And all this because they didn't want me to be like you. They're going to get rid of me because I took after you. If you really think about it, this is all your fault... Thank you, of course, for knocking on the door, but, it was a waste of effort: this time I won't get off that easy... They are determined...

He approaches the UNCLE.

Do you have it?

The UNCLE nods.

Thank you.

The door opens very slowly. MOTHER emerges.

MOTHER
(Quietly.) What are you doing, darling? The food will get cold and then we'll have sulking and whining.

SON
OK – You start and I'll be right there.

MOTHER
I'm waiting.

SON
Not necessary.

MOTHER
You know we won't start without you.

SON
I know, Mummy. I know.

MOTHER
... My darling– How long has it been since you called me that?!

SON
I know... I've caused you a lot of trouble, haven't I?

> *She approaches him.*

MOTHER
Don't worry – these things happen.

SON
... I'm sorry.

> *She embraces him.*

> I really am.

MOTHER
Shhhh... It's over, it's all over now.

SON
... Mummy?

MOTHER
Yes, my darling?

SON
I won't end up in the bathroom, will I?

> *She grabs him by the shoulders.*

MOTHER
(Severely.) Don't ever say that again – don't even think about it.

SON
And everything will be all right?

MOTHER
I promise you.

She kisses him on the forehead. She lets a little sigh escape.

SON
I'll be there in half a minute.

MOTHER
(Smiling.) You better be.

She leaves.

SON
(Quietly.) "You better be"...what do you think? Are they waiting for me behind the door? ... And then again, I can't stay here forever – I am starving... What shall I do?

MOTHER
(Calling from outside.) Time's up.

SON
I'm coming. *(To the UNCLE.)* What you think?

UNCLE produces the knife. He gives it to the SON.

Wish me luck.

He takes a deep breath and exits.

The UNCLE remains alone on the stage.

Charalampos Giannou was born in Cyprus in 1973 and is currently living in Athens, Greece.

He participated in playwriting workshops with Mark Ravenhill (Neue Stucke aus Europa, Wiesbaden, 2010) and Simon Stephens (Obrador d'Estiu-Sala Beckett, Barcelona, 2011). He has also participated in the Playwrights' Studio of the National Theatre of Greece (2015-2016).

His play *Home* will premiere at the New Scene of the National Theater of Greece in April 2017. Other plays of his have been presented at the Contemporary Stage of the National Theatre of Greece, at the New Scene of the Theatrical Organization of Cyprus, at the Teatre Lliure de Barcelona and several other stages.

Hungry received the the Greek State Award for Best Play in 2014, by the Ministry of Culture, Greece. *The Look of Love* received a Distinction at the Theatre Play Contest 2009, by the Theatrical Organization of Cyprus, while *Falling Down the Stairs*, also received a Distinction at the Contest for Young Playwrights 2008, by the National Theatre of Greece.

Plays of his have been translated in English, French, Spanish and Catalan.

His plays include: *The trick to loneliness* (2016), *Some kid* (2016), *Home* (2014), *Hungry* (2012), *the Migrating Woman* (2012), *a doghouse* (2011), *Her life as dead* (2011), *By a thread* (2011), *the Look of Love* (2009), and *Falling Down the Stairs* (2008).

www.ingramcontent.com/pod-product-compliance
Ingram Content Group UK Ltd.
Pitfield, Milton Keynes, MK11 3LW, UK
UKHW031249020325
455689UK00008B/137